James Ramsden is a 27-year-old food writer and broadcaster. He has written about food and cookery for the *Guardian*, the *Times*, the *FT*, *delicious*, *Sainsbury's Magazine*, *London Evening Standard* and many others, and presents the Lad that Lunches on BBC Radio 1. His supper club, the Secret Larder, is one of the most popular in London and was described by one journalist as "harder to get into than the Ivy."

Praise for *Do-ahead Dinners*:

'This is a book you really want. No fifteen-minute magic or culinary sorcery, just practical, staged cooking of the most sumptuous dishes. The style is as lighthearted and enticing as the food. All you need for stress-less kitchen loitering.' *Yotam Ottolenghi*

'James Ramsden's writing is so compelling and his recipes so accessible that *Do-Ahead Dinners* made me want to run straight into the kitchen and start cooking. His is a refreshing, distinctive and authoritative voice in contemporary food writing.' *Russell Norman of Polpo*

'It's fantastic. I want to cook every single thing in it.' *India Knight*

James
Ramsden

creator of
The Secret Larder
supper club

Do-Ahead
DINNERS

How to feed friends and family without the frenzy

Photography by Yuki Sugiura

PAVILION

FOR ROSIE

First published in 2013 by Pavilion Books
10 Southcombe Street, London W14 ORA
An imprint of Anova Books Company Ltd

www.anovabooks.com

ISBN: 9781862059979

A CIP catalogue record for this book is available
from the British Library

10 9 8 7 6 5 4 3 2 1

Reproduction by Mission, Hong Kong
Printed by 1010 Printing International Ltd, China

Commissioning editor: Emily Preece-Morrison
Design & art direction: Georgina Hewitt
Photographer: Yuki Sugiura
Home economist: Valerie Berry
Stylist: Wei Tang
Copy editor: Maggie Ramsay

NOTES
1 teaspoon = 5ml; 1 tablespoon = 15ml.
All spoon measurements are level.
Both metric and imperial measures are given
for the recipes. Follow either set of measures,
not a mixture of both, as they are not
interchangeable. Medium eggs should be
used, except where otherwise specified.
Free-range eggs are recommended.
Note that some recipes contain raw or
lightly cooked eggs. The young, elderly,
pregnant women and anyone with an
immune-deficiency disease should avoid
these, because of the slight risk of salmonella.

To sterilize jars for pickles, sauces and jams,
put the jars in a preheated oven at
150°C/300°F/Gas mark 2 for 20 minutes.

Contents

INTRODUCTION

The Secret Larder supper club was born in the spring of 2010, perhaps a month after my sister and I had moved into the chemistry classroom in a converted schoolhouse, and a year after the London supper club movement had begun to take shape. These were informal restaurants crowbarred into people's living rooms and kitchens, helmed by chefs on sabbatical or, as in my case, enthusiastic cooks.

There was, I suppose, no great concept. I wanted an excuse to cook for lots of people on a regular basis and my sister Mary was happy to play front-of-house. We'd exhibit different artists and photographers, rope in friends to help in return for food and wine, and base menus on whim or weather.

Before we knew it, powered by social media and some vigorous emailing, we were booked up for the next few months, despite no one yet having actually eaten any of the food or assessed the ricketiness of the furniture. I soon realized that as far as the food was concerned, the only way to feed twenty people four courses, with one oven and four hobs, and in full view of everyone (it's an open kitchen, so no hiding from guests or putting dropped food back on plates), was to cook as much as possible in advance.

This wasn't the restriction it first seemed. It meant I could be organized hours before the first knock on the door, it meant I could talk to guests when they arrived instead of being wedged in the kitchen, and it meant that the experience of feeding a bunch of strangers was, far from being an ordeal, enormous fun.

It was a theory that was put most rigorously to the test when we moved the supper club to Printers and Stationers, a wine shop in East London with all the atmosphere we could have hoped for, but nothing that really resembled a kitchen. So now I cook everything at home, chuck it in the back of the car, and turn up just in time to stick on an apron and dish up.

I'm becoming increasingly convinced that this is the ideal way for anyone to cook for guests, as it eliminates one of the greatest stresses of feeding people – that of being in a deranged flap when it comes to dinner. This way, instead of being the stereotypical panicked and mucky-aproned host when your friends arrive clutching bottles and shaking umbrellas, you are in a state of complete control and composure. You can mix drinks, dish out something to nibble on, and actually have a conversation with your guests.

The cooking side of things becomes so much more enjoyable, too. You are not cooking against the clock or racing anyone, but rather taking things at your own pace and on your own terms. It is you who is in charge, not the recipe writer.

THE RECIPES

This is the food I like to cook, the food I want to eat. It is home cooking with perhaps only the slightest swagger – simple recipes with just enough of a twist to lift them above the quotidian.

Each recipe is divided into sections according to what you can do ahead, and what you need to do to complete the dish before serving. (This is not a book of lasagnes and cottage pies – there will, with many of these recipes, be a couple of things that need doing to finish each dish. My aim is to keep cooking for friends as stress-free as possible, eliminating the scope for last-minute cock-ups while maintaining a sense of freshness and, I suppose, modernity.) Of course, such a system is not exhaustive. There is nothing stopping you from sweating some onions and then buggering off for four hours before continuing with a dish. But it would be nigh on impossible for me – and impossibly dull for you – to cover every eventuality. I've tried to break recipes up into natural stages.

The most important thing is to read a recipe in full before you start cooking, in order to work out the best way forward for you.

As for the kit required, well, there's nothing out of the ordinary. I use an ice-cream machine but it's not essential; a food processor is handy but you can largely get by without one; a blender is useful for soups – a handheld stick blender works just as well and is much cheaper. I'm afraid it's really just the old clichés of a decent sharp knife and a couple of solid saucepans that I'd view as, if not quite essential, at least more efficient than a dull knife and flimsy pans. Oh, and bowls. You can never have too many bowls. Because you're preparing food in advance, you're going to need somewhere to store it, and a good set of mixing bowls that stack neatly in a cupboard will be your best friend.

I have cooked all of these recipes in one form or another for twenty people at the Secret Larder. None of them is outrageously complex or challenging. Some are relatively quick to throw together, and others take a little longer. In the age of the 15-minute meal, I'd say this is no bad thing.

PLANNING A MENU

First of all I would urge you not to feel as if you have to serve three or four courses. Many of these dishes happily stand alone – a soup for a midweek supper, a roast pork belly for Sunday lunch – and so there's no need for a banquet if you lack the time or energy. But should you decide to roast the whole hog, then there are one or two things to keep in mind.

You need a menu that is practical. As important as dishes that work together in terms of balance and flavour, are dishes for which you have the right kit and crockery. So if you only have one large saucepan, then make sure your menu doesn't require three. Create a menu with a balance of cold and hot dishes, so that you're not trying to keep ten things warm at once. If your starter requires the use of the grill, then make sure the oven isn't already spoken for. This sort of planning will help to make your dinner run seamlessly.

As for the food itself, I'm reluctant to prescribe full menus – you know what you like and what you feel you can cook – though there are a few suggestions on p.234 should you need some inspiration. Really you're just looking for a balance of lightness and colour, of texture and temperature. Go with your gut.

MULTIPLICATION

The majority of recipes serve between four and eight people. Halving recipes is generally a straightforward operation. But if you're multiplying, particularly several times, it's worth taking a second to consider which ingredients don't need direct multiplication. For example, if you are doing three times a risotto recipe, you will need three times the amount of rice, but you won't necessarily need to bulk the onion and celery up by so much, and you certainly won't need to double the amount of oil. It's rarely disastrous if you do in fact whack everything up several times (though careful with chillies), but you can save yourself time and money by being judicious.

IF YOU NEED HELP

If you have any questions or concerns, please do get in touch, either via email – james@jamesramsden.com – or Twitter @jteramsden, or using the hashtag #dogheaddinners

Bread

Bread is gloriously easy to make. It costs little to produce, requires hardly any skill, and it does most of the hard work itself. And yet who isn't impressed when they encounter a homemade loaf?

It's also the height of do-aheadability – not something to embark upon half an hour before your guests turn up. Do it in the morning – or the night before at a push – and you'll have beautifully fresh bread for your supper. Don't get distracted by romantic notions of bread 'fresh from the oven', for a still-warm loaf is not a finished loaf, and will be too doughy in the middle. Serve the bread warm by all means, but warm it up again in the oven.

I should probably qualify the suggestion that bread requires little skill by saying that my sort of bread – rustic, amateur, home-spun – at any rate requires only a pinch of nous. Far be it from me to denigrate the remarkable abilities of the professional baker. Once you've got the hang of how dough behaves you can then, if you wish, start delving into the amazing world of natural yeast – and there are people far more qualified than I in this field (books by Richard Bertinet and Dan Lepard are good places to start) – but when you've got people coming round and you just fancy throwing a loaf together, then this is the sort of thing to go for. These are teary-sharey breads, good for dunking and scooping and mopping.

OTHER TIPS
- A dough spatula and a dough cutter/scraper will be your best friends, the former for scooping dough from bowls, the second for cutting and shaping.
- I find it better to have wet, not floured, hands when working with dough. Oiled hands work well, too.
- Trust your instincts – bread is a living, wilful thing, so a recipe will never be 100 per cent foolproof. If I say leave for an hour but the dough looks ready after 45 minutes, go for it.

YEAST

These breads use dried yeast, purely because it's easier to find. Most bakers can give you fresh yeast, if you prefer to use this. You'll need about double the amount, and should whisk it into the warm water called for in the recipe. Leave for 10 minutes before using.

TO KNEAD BREAD

As with most things in cooking, there is more than one way to skin a cat, and where one person will tell you to slap the dough about like a wet towel, another will tell you to leave it altogether. Ultimately you're trying to develop the gluten and begin the fermentation process. So, this is how I do it:

Tip the dough onto a very lightly floured surface. Put your left hand on the edge of the dough nearest you to anchor it, then using the heel of your right hand, push the furthest side of the dough away from you, stretching it as you do so. With your right hand, fold the dough back over itself, turn 90 degrees and repeat. Keep doing this until the dough is smooth and springy, which will usually take about 10 minutes.

BREAD ROLLS

MAKES 8–10 ROLLS
200g/7oz/generous 1½ cups
     strong white bread flour
200g/7oz/generous 1½ cups
     strong wholemeal
     (whole wheat) flour
7g/¼oz (1 sachet) fast-action
     dried yeast
1 tsp fine salt
275ml/9½fl oz/scant 1¼ cups
     warm water

These are dead easy to make and just what you want for tearing and decadently slathering with butter. As with most bread, these rolls are best eaten on the day they're baked, though they can be made a day or two ahead.

UP TO 12 HOURS AHEAD:

Mix the flours, yeast and salt in a large bowl and make a well in the centre. Pour in the warm water and mix together by hand until combined, then tip onto a lightly floured surface and knead for 7–10 minutes until smooth and elastic. Transfer to a clean bowl, cover with a tea towel and leave to rise in a warm place for 1 hour, until doubled in size.

Flour a work surface and gently tip the dough onto it. Divide into 8–10 balls. Place on a floured baking sheet with space between the balls, cover with a tea towel and leave for 30 minutes.

Preheat the oven to 220°C/425°F/Gas mark 7. Bake the rolls for 20 minutes. They're done when they feel light and, when tapped on the bottom, sound hollow. Cool on a wire rack.

TART: If you like a slightly richer dough, mix in a little melted butter when you add the water.
TWEAK: For white bread rolls, use all white flour.
TOMORROW: These will keep in a bread bin for a couple of days, and freeze very well.

CIABATTA

MAKES 2 LOAVES

For the pre-ferment

250g/9oz/2 cups plain
(all purpose) flour

250ml/9fl oz/generous 1 cup
warm water

a pinch of fast-action
dried yeast

For the loaves

500g/1lb 2oz/4 cups plain
(all-purpose) flour

½ tsp fast-action dried yeast

2 tsp fine salt

350ml/12fl oz/1½ cups warm
water

This loaf uses what is known as a *biga* starter, a sort of night-before pre-ferment operation which takes all of 5 seconds to make but means you get a light and billowy and chewy loaf. It's a cheat's sourdough starter, really. The bread is baked on the day you want to eat it, but you can fit it into your cooking schedule. Plan to use the oven for something else once the bread is done.

THE NIGHT BEFORE:
Whisk together the flour, water and yeast for the pre-ferment until smooth. Let it sit for 10 minutes, then cover with a tea towel and leave at room temperature for at least 6 hours or overnight.

UP TO 12 HOURS AHEAD:
For the loaves, put the flour in a large bowl with the yeast and salt, then mix in the pre-ferment. Slowly mix in the warm water and, when all is incorporated, tip onto a lightly floured surface and knead for 8–10 minutes until you have a smooth, sticky dough. Transfer to a clean bowl, cover with a tea towel and leave to rise in a warm place for 1 hour, until doubled in size.

Flour a work surface and gently tip the dough onto it. Cut in half and with lightly floured hands shape into 2 long loaves. Cover and leave for 30 minutes.

Meanwhile, preheat the oven to 240°C/475°F/Gas mark 9 and lightly flour a large baking sheet.

Put the loaves onto the baking sheet. Bake for 20–25 minutes, until golden. Cool on a wire rack.

TART: Mix some chopped black olives through the dough half-way through kneading.

TWEAK: For a wholemeal ciabatta use half wholemeal flour and half plain flour.

TOMORROW: Use leftover bread to make panzanella (p.71) or crostini.

RED ONION AND ROSEMARY FOCACCIA

MAKES 1 THICK LOAF

500g/1lb 2oz/4 cups plain
(all-purpose) flour

2 tsp salt

7g/¼oz (1 sachet) fast-action
dried yeast

325ml/11fl oz/scant 1½ cups
warm water

4 tsp olive oil

To finish

olive oil

2 tbsp dry white wine
(optional)

1 red onion, peeled, sliced
and gently fried until soft

a handful of rosemary sprigs

a good pinch of sea salt

I love the juiciness and stickiness of this loaf, as well as its amazing versatility. It's ideal for tearing apart and dipping into olive oil, but you can also bulk up the toppings and turn it into something of a pizza.

Focaccia is best eaten the day it's made, but there's plenty of rising time during which you can be getting on with other elements of the dinner – hands-on time is minimal.

6–12 HOURS AHEAD:

Mix the flour, salt and yeast in a large bowl and make a well in the centre. Add the warm water and olive oil and, using your hand like a claw, mix together thoroughly. Tip onto a lightly floured surface and knead for 10 minutes, until smooth and elastic. Transfer to a clean bowl and cover with a tea towel. Put in a warm place away from any draught and leave for an hour or so, until doubled in size.

Line a 20 x 30cm/8 x 12in baking sheet with baking parchment. Oil the parchment and tip the dough onto it. Use your fingertips to manipulate the dough out to the edges. It will rebel, but fear not – do your best, then cover it with a tea towel and leave for 30 minutes.

Drizzle with a good amount of olive oil and white wine, then stretch out the dough again to the edges, creating plenty of troughs for the oil to collect in. Scatter over the onion and rosemary and finish with sea salt. Leave, uncovered, in a warm place for 1 hour, or a cool place for 3 hours, until well risen. If it starts to look too dry, sprinkle with tepid water.

Preheat the oven to 220°C/425°F/Gas mark 7. Bake the focaccia for 10 minutes, then turn the oven down to 190°C/375°F/Gas mark 5 and bake for a further 15 minutes, until golden. Cool on a wire rack.

TART: For more of a pizza focaccia you can top with chopped olives, Taleggio cheese, sun-dried tomatoes – whatever you like on pizza, really.

TWEAK: Instead of red onion and rosemary, go for the more classic white onion and sage.

TOMORROW: Eat within a day, or toast stale focaccia and use as a base for bruschetta topped with chopped tomatoes and basil.

FOUGASSE WITH OLIVES AND ANCHOVIES

MAKES 1 LARGE LOAF

500g/1lb 2oz/4 cups strong white bread flour

7g/¼oz (1 sachet) fast-action dried yeast

a pinch of salt

300ml/10fl oz/1¼ cups warm water

35g/1¼oz anchovies, finely chopped

70g/2½oz black olives, pitted and finely chopped

1 tsp finely chopped thyme leaves

Fougasse, a close relative of the Italian focaccia (p.13), comes from Provence, where they like to slash the bread to make it resemble an ear of wheat.

UP TO 12 HOURS AHEAD:

Sift the flour into a large bowl and mix in the yeast and salt. Make a well in the centre and tip in the water. Using your hand like a claw, mix until smooth and uniform. Tip onto a lightly floured surface and knead for 5 minutes. Add the anchovies, olives and thyme and knead for a further 3 minutes until smooth, elastic and not too sticky. Transfer to a clean bowl, cover with a tea towel and leave to rise in a warm place for 45 minutes.

Flour a baking sheet and turn the dough out onto it. Flatten it into an oblong shape and make a long, deep slash down the centre, then three diagonal slashes on each side, to resemble an ear of wheat. Prise the slashes open with your fingers – be quite assertive – cover the dough with a tea towel and leave to rise in a warm place for 30 minutes.

Preheat the oven to 250°C/500°F/Gas mark 10. Put the fougasse on the middle shelf and throw a glass of water into the bottom of the oven. This creates steam and stops a crust forming too quickly on the dough. Bake for 20 minutes, until golden brown. Cool on a wire rack.

TART: A good grating of Gruyère cheese before the bread goes in the oven would be a decadent touch.

TWEAK: Instead of the anchovies, add little strips of crisply fried bacon.

LAVASH

MAKES 6 PIECES

400g/14oz/3¼ cups plain
(all-purpose) flour
1 tsp fine salt
1 tsp caster (superfine) sugar
125ml/4fl oz/½ cup warm
water
1 egg white
2 tbsp olive oil
To finish
1 egg white, beaten
a handful of sesame seeds

I am addicted to Turkish food in all its forms – the meat roasted over open flames, the salads all perky with sumac and lemon, the sticky, sweet pastries, and the smoky, tearable breads. Lavash, a Middle Eastern flatbread, is part bread, part cutlery. When faced with a plate of roasted meats and yogurt and herbs all hugger-mugger, you can forget your knife and fork – just tear and scoop.

You can make these several hours in advance, but do keep them well wrapped in tea towels to prevent them from drying out.

UP TO 6 HOURS AHEAD:

Preheat the oven to 250°C/500°F/Gas mark 10.

Put the flour, salt and sugar in a large bowl and mix thoroughly. Add the water, egg white and olive oil, and mix until combined, then tip onto a lightly floured surface and knead for 5 minutes, until smooth. Cover with a tea towel and leave to rest for 5 minutes.

Divide the dough into 6 balls. On a lightly floured surface, roll out a couple of balls until almost paper-thin and place on a baking sheet (keep the others covered). Brush with egg white and sprinkle with sesame seeds, then bake for 4–5 minutes until golden and slightly puffed. Repeat for the remaining dough. When all the breads are done, wrap in a tea towel or two until ready to serve.

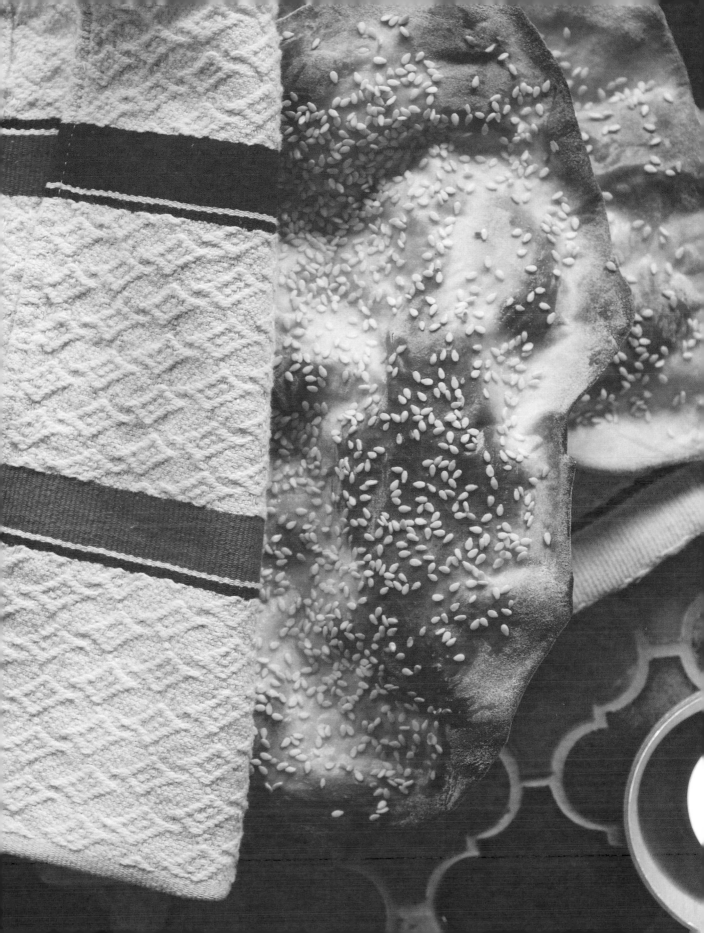

SPICED FLATBREADS

MAKES 8 BREADS

1 tsp coriander seeds

1 tsp fennel seeds

1 tsp black onion seeds

½ tsp cumin

¼ tsp chilli flakes

500g/1lb 2oz/4 cups strong white bread flour

7g/¼oz (1 sachet) fast-action dried yeast

1 tsp fine salt

350ml/12fl oz/1½ cups warm water

These are really just a doughier, turbo version of the lavash (p.16). The dough here is leavened, and has the added oomph of spice, but the breads essentially perform the same job at the table – that of scooping up goodies like baba ganoush (p.23), or of being stuffed with meat and salad and yogurt.

UP TO 6 HOURS AHEAD:

In a dry frying pan, toast the coriander, fennel, onion and cumin seeds over a medium heat for a minute, shaking occasionally. Tip into a pestle and mortar and roughly crush.

In a large bowl, mix the crushed spices and chilli flakes through the flour, along with the yeast and the salt. Make a well in the centre and add the water. Stir to combine, then tip onto a lightly floured surface and knead for 8–10 minutes until smooth and elastic. Cover and leave for 30 minutes.

Put a non-stick frying pan over a medium-high heat. Divide the dough into 8 pieces and, on a lightly floured surface, roll out into slipper shapes. Cook for 3 minutes on each side, one or two at a time (depending on the size of your pan). If they char slightly, all the better. Wrap in a tea towel and keep covered until ready to serve.

TWEAK: Instead of the spices used above, use a couple of spoonfuls of dukkah (p.30).

TOMORROW: Leftovers can be cut up, fried and served in a Middle Eastern-style *fattoush* salad with cucumber, radish, tomatoes, onion... it's a pretty flexible dish.

RYE BREAD

MAKES 1 LOAF

500g/1lb 2oz/4 cups rye flour

2 tbsp dark brown sugar

2 tsp salt

7g/¼oz (1 sachet) fast-action dried yeast

1 tbsp lightly crushed caraway seeds

350ml/12fl oz/1½ cups warm water

My penchant for pickled fish and general Scandi fare dictates that a dark and sweet rye bread recipe is absolutely necessary. Best toasted, in my opinion, so it won't suffer from being kept in a bread bin for a couple of days, or frozen. Serve with soused herring (p.84) or cured salmon (p.83).

UP TO A DAY AHEAD:

Mix the flour, sugar, salt, yeast and caraway seeds in a large bowl. Make a well in the centre and add the water. Stir to combine, then tip onto a lightly floured surface and knead for 10 minutes, until firm and elastic. It will be quite sticky. Transfer to a clean bowl, cover with a tea towel and leave to rise in a warm place for 1 hour, until well risen.

Carefully tip onto a floured baking sheet and shape into a round loaf. It should be firm and hold its shape. If it doesn't, then return it to the covered bowl and let it ferment for longer. Cover the loaf with a tea towel and leave for 30 minutes.

Meanwhile, preheat the oven to 250°C/500°F/Gas mark 10.

Slash the loaf once or twice with a sharp knife, then put it on the middle shelf of the oven, chucking a glass of water into the bottom of the oven to create steam and prevent a crust from forming too quickly on the dough. Bake for 10 minutes, then turn the oven down to 200°C/400°F/Gas mark 6 and bake for another 15–20 minutes. The loaf is done if the bottom sounds hollow when tapped. Leave on a wire rack to cool completely before serving.

TWEAK: This makes quite a dark, sticky loaf. For something lighter and more suited to, say, sandwiches, use half rye and half strong white bread flour, and omit the sugar.

Small nibbles

These are not canapés. There's no food in miniature or tweezered presentation – just big, punchy flavours and plenty of salt and spice and crunch. Some of these recipes are quick and straight-forward, while others take a little more time. They are all here because the result is worth every minute of prep required.

There is nothing really wrong with a bowl of crisps, but these show extra effort, love, care and generosity – for what could demonstrate more succinctly your willingness to spoil your friends than a soft-yolked, hot, crispy Scotch egg?

Dipping and scooping

Dips and the like are ideal in a do-ahead world. Notwithstanding the bagna cauda on p.24, they can usually be done well in advance, leaving you safe in the knowledge that you've got something with which you can feed your guests as soon as they have a drink in their hand.

ANCHOÏADE

MAKES 300ML/10FL OZ/ 1¼ CUPS

100g/3½oz jar of anchovies, drained (and rinsed, if salted)
a bunch of parsley, leaves only (no need to be too fussy about stalks)
a sprig of rosemary, needles only, roughly chopped
1 garlic clove, peeled and roughly chopped
a good squeeze of lemon juice
1 tsp orange blossom water (optional but recommended)
100ml/3½fl oz/6–7 tbsp olive oil
pepper

This is as good a celebration of the anchovy as I know, and a complete treat for any ancho-addicts. For those who are more suspicious of the unmistakably assertive fish, I reckon this Provençal dip has the ability to convert them.

You can make it a day or two ahead. It's delicious served with warm bread or crisp vegetables, radishes being a personal favourite; wash and prep the vegetables up to 12 hours before dinnertime.

UP TO A DAY AHEAD:
Put the anchovies, herbs, garlic, lemon juice and orange blossom water in a food processor and blend. Alternatively, mash together using a pestle and mortar, or chop together with a sharp knife and then put in a bowl. Slowly blend or stir in the olive oil and taste for seasoning. It may warrant a scrunch of pepper, though it is unlikely to need salt. Cover and chill.

1 HOUR BEFORE SERVING:
Take the anchoïade out of the fridge. Serve at room temperature on toasted bread or with chunks of focaccia, or, as is more traditional, with some raw vegetables.

TART: The orange blossom water is a transformative tarting option, but you could also bung in some chopped shallot to give it a little more bite.
TWEAK: Play around with the herbs, adding a little tarragon, chervil, chive, mint or whatever you fancy.
TOMORROW: It's best eaten within 24 hours, though will keep for a few days in the fridge, covered with a layer of olive oil.

BABA GANOUSH WITH PARSLEY OIL

SERVES 6–8

olive oil

1 onion, peeled and finely chopped

1 garlic clove, peeled and finely chopped

2 aubergines (eggplants), pricked a few times with a fork

1 tbsp sesame paste (tahini)

juice of ½ lemon

salt and pepper

For the parsley oil

a bunch of parsley

100ml/3½fl oz/6–7 tbsp olive oil

a good squeeze of lemon juice

It's all about the smoke, this dish. If you lose your nerve for fear of burning the aubergine, you won't achieve the same deep, bonfired richness that the best baba ganoushes carry. Other than that It's very simple, and indeed will improve by being done a day or two ahead. The parsley oil is perhaps a little precious for some, and can be omitted, but I like the colour and the zippy edge it brings.

UP TO 3 DAYS AHEAD:

Heat a good slosh of oil in a pan and gently cook the onion and garlic until softened. Set aside.

Whack a couple of gas flames on high and put the aubergines directly on top. Alternatively, if, like me, you don't have gas, put the aubergines under a very hot grill. Cook for about 20 minutes, turning every couple of minutes but letting the skin char well. Once soft, run under a cold tap and remove the skin and stalks.

Put the aubergines in a blender and add the onion, garlic, tahini and lemon juice. Season with salt and pepper, and blend until smooth. Taste for seasoning, cover and chill. (If you don't have a blender, use a potato masher.)

UP TO 2 HOURS AHEAD:

To make the parsley oil, finely chop the parsley and stir in the olive oil, a pinch of salt and a good squeeze of lemon juice.

1 HOUR BEFORE SERVING:

Take the baba ganoush out of the fridge. Drizzle with the parsley oil and serve at room temperature with warm flatbreads (p.18), pitta breads or fresh vegetables.

TART: Add 1 tsp toasted and crushed cumin and/or coriander seeds to the baba ganoush.

TWEAK: Use a handful of fresh rocket instead of parsley.

TOMORROW: The baba ganoush will keep for several days in the fridge, as will the parsley oil, although the oil will lose its vibrant colour after a while.

BAGNA CAUDA WITH RAW VEGETABLES

SERVES 4–6

1 garlic clove
100g/3½oz jar of anchovies, drained (and rinsed, if salted)
3 tbsp olive oil
50g/1¾oz/4 tbsp butter, softened
pepper

For the vegetables
1 fennel bulb
a handful of radishes
1 head of chicory
a bunch of spring onions (scallions)
a few beetroot

Bagna cauda isn't a million miles away from anchoïade (p.22), hailing from just over the border in Italy, and containing the mighty anchovy as its principal ingredient. But it's served warm, and has the added richness of butter. It is best when its hot, salty, buttery depths rub shoulders with the fresh, cold crunch of raw vegetables such as fennel, radish and chicory. The pungent aromas of anchovies and garlic can linger on your fingers, so it's good to get the chopping done ahead of time.

UP TO 12 HOURS AHEAD:

You can prep the vegetables well ahead of time, though be aware that fennel and radish in particular like the cold. Slice the fennel thickly and leave in a bowl of cold water in the fridge with the radishes and a squeeze of lemon juice (this prevents the fennel from discolouring). Wash the chicory leaves and spring onions and refrigerate. Peel and slice the beetroot, cover and refrigerate.

Peel and crush the garlic and finely chop the anchovies. Put them in a small bowl, cover and set aside until needed.

30 MINUTES AHEAD:

Warm a bowl in a low oven.

Drain the fennel and radishes and arrange in a bowl or on a plate along with the other vegetables.

In a small pan, warm the oil over a medium-low heat and add the anchovies and garlic. Stir for a few minutes until smooth and emulsified, then whisk in the softened butter a piece at a time until fully incorporated and smooth. Taste for seasoning and keep warm over a very low heat, stirring regularly. When ready to serve, give it a brief whisk, then tip into the warmed bowl and serve with the vegetables.

TWEAK: Some warm ciabatta (p.11) would be a useful tool for mopping up leftovers.
TOMORROW: Stir leftover bagna cauda through hot spaghetti along with a pinch of chilli flakes.

CHORIZO
CHEESE TWISTS

MAKES 12 STRAWS
375g/13oz puff pastry
2 tbsp whole milk
a good handful of grated
    Parmesan cheese
75g/2¾oz thinly sliced chorizo
1 egg, beaten

These come courtesy of my friend Annabel Partridge, who along with her sister Charlotte runs a supper club called Supper in a Pear Tree. Charlotte holds a life drawing class before dinner, during which you slurp wine and try your best at rendering a naked body, and then Annabel cooks dinner. Wine, nudity and food – what's not to like?

These are a sort of tarted-up cheese straw. Irresistible nibbly things that I often serve alongside a vegetable soup, such as pea and courgette (p.56) or celeriac (p.50).

UP TO 12 HOURS AHEAD:
Preheat the oven to 180°C/350°F/Gas mark 4. Line a baking sheet with a piece of baking parchment.

Cut the puff pastry in half and roll out both pieces on a lightly floured surface, making two equal-sized rectangles. Brush one piece with milk, leaving a 1cm/½in border all round, then scatter the cheese over the pastry. Lay the slices of chorizo on top, still leaving a small gap around the edge, then brush this border with beaten egg.

Put the other piece of pastry on top and press to seal the edge. Brush all over with beaten egg, then slice into 12 strips. Twist the strips around a few times, then place on the baking sheet. Bake for 15–17 minutes, until golden. Serve warm or cold.

TART: Mix a pinch of hot smoked paprika through the Parmesan.
TWEAK: Replace the Parmesan and chorizo with Gruyère and anchovy, and instead of cutting up and twisting, bake the pastry whole and cut into pieces afterwards.

PORK SCRATCHINGS WITH GUACAMOLE

MAKES 40 SCRATCHINGS

about 500g/1lb 2oz pigskin
    from the belly or shoulder
a handful of fine salt
For the guacamole
2 ripe avocados
½ red onion, peeled and
    finely chopped
1 red chilli, deseeded and
    finely chopped
1 ripe tomato, finely chopped
juice of 1 lime
a small bunch of coriander
    (cilantro), roughly chopped
salt and pepper

Pigskin is an extraordinarily cheap commodity, if you can find it. After all, it tends not to have its own section in the supermarket, which, in turn, is probably why it's so cheap. Give your local butcher a day or two's warning and he or she should be able to help, if not give the stuff away. Alternatively, buy a piece of pork belly and remove the skin, using the meat for the potted pork (p.92).

Guacamole will turn a dingy grey colour if left for more than about 2 hours, but you can get your scratchings stashed a day or so ahead.

UP TO A DAY AHEAD (THOUGH THE SCRATCHINGS ARE ALSO EXCELLENT SERVED WARM):

Trim the skin of excess fat and shave off any hairy bits. Scatter the skin side all over with fine salt. This leaches out any excess water, making for a crispier scratching. Leave for 1 hour until the skin is dappled with moisture.

Preheat the oven to 160°C/325°F/Gas mark 3. Pat the skin thoroughly dry and, using your sharpest knife, cut into whatever shapes you fancy. I favour long and slender, like crackling, to serve with the guacamole. Place on a baking sheet and bake for about 45 minutes, or until thoroughly golden and blistered. Remove from the oven and leave to cool. Store in an airtight container.

UP TO 2 HOURS BEFORE SERVING:

Peel and stone the avocados and mash with the other ingredients in a pestle and mortar, or in a bowl, using a potato masher. Taste for seasoning and add a little salt and more lime juice if necessary. Cover.

DINNERTIME:

Serve the scratchings with the guacamole.

TART: Brine the skin first: dissolve 400g salt in 5 litres water and add crushed coriander seeds, juniper berries, a bay leaf and a few sprigs of thyme. Leave the skin in the brine for a day, then rinse thoroughly, pat dry and proceed as above.

TWEAK: Omit the scratchings and serve the guacamole with tortilla chips.

TOMORROW: The scratchings will keep in an airtight container for a few days, although they're best when fresh and, let's face it, are unlikely to stick around for long.

DUKKAH

SERVES 4–6

2 tsp cumin seeds

4 tsp coriander seeds

1 tsp black onion seeds
   (kalonji or nigella)

1 tbsp za'atar

1 tbsp finely chopped
   pistachios

1 tbsp finely chopped
   hazelnuts

½ tsp sea salt

freshly ground pepper

This is an extraordinarily evocative and aromatic spice and nut mix that originated in Egypt. Za'atar is a herb mix containing sumac, thyme or oregano, sesame seeds and salt; these days you can find it in most supermarkets. Use whole spices, as you're not looking for a powder here, but a rough mixture that crunches in the mouth. It's intoxicating stuff. In theory this will keep forever, but it's a dish of diminishing returns, and is better when at its most fresh – up to three days is fine.

Serve in a shallow bowl, with good bread and olive oil, dunking the bread first in the oil and then in the dukkah.

UP TO 3 DAYS AHEAD:

Put a frying pan over a medium heat – no oil – and add the spices and nuts. Some would recommend that you do the spices one at a time as they toast at different rates. This may be sensible, but quite frankly I wouldn't bother and wouldn't expect you to. Keep a close eye on the pan and you shouldn't burn the things.

So, pan on heat, spices in, and shake the pan almost continuously until the kitchen smells like a souk. Tip into a mortar and pound until broken down but not powdery. Season with salt and pepper to taste and store in an airtight jar in the fridge.

TART: For a pretty, Middle Eastern touch, add dried rose petals to the mix after grinding the spices.

TWEAK: If you can't find za'atar, then replace with sesame seeds and a pinch of dried oregano. You could leave out the pistachios, which can be quite expensive, and double the hazelnut quotient.

Down-in-one things

These morsels are less involved for the cook and quite shovelable for the guest – ideal if the rest of your menu contains several last-minute bits and pieces.

ROASTED SPICED ALMONDS

SERVES 8–10
200g/7oz almonds
1 tsp olive oil
1 tsp hot smoked paprika
a good pinch of ground cumin
½ tsp sea salt

Salty, crunchy and spicy – perfect drinking snacks, these. They will keep happily in a jar for some time, but will lose their oomph after a while.

UP TO A WEEK AHEAD:
Preheat the oven to 140°C/275°F/Gas mark 1. Toss all the ingredients together, tip into a roasting pan and roast for 40 minutes. Serve warm or cold.

TART: I've been relatively conservative with the spicing here – you could try adding ground coriander, garlic powder and cayenne.
TWEAK: Although the paprika gives a smokiness of its own, almonds are a good starting point for home smoking. Get some fine oak chips from a garden centre and put them in a roasting pan with a fine-meshed rack over the top. Scatter the almonds on the rack and cover tightly with foil. Put over a medium heat and, once it starts smoking, turn the heat down and smoke for 10 minutes.

RADISHES WITH BUTTER AND SALT

SERVES 4
a bunch of radishes
decent butter
Maldon sea salt

OK, so this is less a recipe than an idea, but it's not necessarily something you'd think of doing, and is a bit of a treat, and a frugal treat at that. If you can, buy long, leafy, French breakfast radishes, whose pinky blush belies a pleasingly eye-watering heat.

UP TO A DAY AHEAD:
Wash any dirt off the radishes. Store in the fridge.

UP TO AN HOUR AHEAD:
Drop the radishes into a bowl of iced water to help make them super-crunchy. Leave until ready to eat. Dip the roots first into soft, golden butter, and then into salt, and then finally into your mouth. Save the leaves for salad.

RAMERINO
IN CULO

MAKES 12
300g/10½oz good beef rump
salt and pepper
6 sprigs of rosemary, halved
olive oil
sea salt, to serve

I find it faintly irritating when cookery writers precede recipes with a story about how they first encountered such and such a dish in a tiny restaurant in some remote village in Tuscany that no one had before or has since visited, but it would be naughty of me not to acknowledge the provenance of this recipe.

I first encountered this dish in a remote village in Tuscany at a restaurant run by a singing butcher called Dario. He called it *ramerino in culo*, *ramerino* being Tuscan for rosemary, and *culo* being Italian for arse, and... well, you can work out the rest.

UP TO 8 HOURS AHEAD:
Chop the meat finely or pulse it in a blender, though be careful not to over-blend it – you're looking for a coarser consistency than mince. Season with salt and pepper to taste. Form into 12 balls. Place on a plate, flattening the bottom a little, then push a sprig of rosemary into each ball, pressing the meat in around it. Cover and chill.

30 MINUTES AHEAD:
Remove from the fridge: it's crucial that the meat is at room temperature before cooking.

DINNERTIME:
Heat a little oil in a non-stick frying pan over a high heat. Add the meatballs and cook for 1–2 minutes, until the bottom is nicely caramelized but the top is still raw. Sprinkle with sea salt and serve.

Hot and crispy things

The hot, salty crunch of something that has just emerged from a bubbling cauldron of oil is perhaps the finest accompaniment to a drink that there is. Whether a bowl of fat Scotch eggs, savoury rissoles, or oozing croquettes, few things beat fried treats when it comes to nibbling and sipping.

You can find decent deep-fat fryers for about the same price as a leg of lamb these days, but finding somewhere to store one is perhaps more tricky. Most of the time, I just use a saucepan of oil – you can check the temperature using a cooks' thermometer, or just based on how long it takes a piece of bread to colour.

Oil for deep-frying should be used once only. To dispose of the oil, leave it to cool in a safe place, tip it into an old bottle and bin it.

SCOTCH QUAIL EGGS WITH BROWN SAUCE

Is there a food that has suffered more of a fall from grace than the Scotch egg? A thing of perfection, sadly reduced to the status of petrol station junk. Thankfully, they've seen a resurgence of late, and Scotch eggs are now, arguably, the king of pub snacks.

There are several things to remember when making your own. Firstly, your eggs don't want to be too fresh, otherwise they'll be a swine to peel. Secondly, to ensure a soft yolk, they do need to be served fairly soon after cooking. Thirdly, this recipe takes a certain degree of patience and commitment, though with hand on heart, I can honestly say it's worth every ruddy second – and you can do so much of it in advance that when you come to cook the things you'll have forgotten about the prep.

If you don't have time to make the brown sauce then shop-bought will do the trick. This recipe makes enough to go with the eggs, though it's certainly worth making a bigger batch if you're a voracious brown sauce eater.

See p.36 for ingredients and method.

MAKES 12

12 quail eggs

6 plump sausages – about 500g/1lb 2oz

2 tsp finely chopped thyme

2 tsp finely chopped tarragon

2 sage leaves, finely chopped

1 tbsp finely chopped parsley

½ tsp crushed fennel seeds

½ tsp crushed celery seeds (optional)

salt and pepper

For coating and deep-frying

3 tbsp plain (all-purpose) flour, seasoned with salt and pepper

2 eggs, lightly beaten

50g/1¾oz/½ cup fine dried breadcrumbs

1 litre/1¾ pints/4 cups vegetable oil

For the brown sauce

olive oil

1 onion, peeled and finely chopped

1 garlic clove, peeled and crushed

200ml/7fl oz/generous ¾ cup tomato ketchup

4 tbsp malt vinegar

2 tbsp tamarind

½ tsp ground ginger

a pinch of ground cloves

AS FAR AHEAD AS YOU LIKE:

Make the brown sauce: heat a little oil in a saucepan over a low heat, add the onion and garlic and cook until softened, then add the remaining ingredients and season with salt and pepper. Simmer for 15 minutes, until thickened. Pass through a sieve, cool, and store in a sterilized jar (see note on p.2) in the fridge. It will keep for up to 6 months.

UP TO A DAY AHEAD:

Fill a bowl with cold water and ice. Bring a pan of water to a boil and carefully drop in the quail eggs. Boil for 2 minutes, then transfer to the iced water and set aside.

Skin the sausages and mix with the herbs and spices, along with a pinch of salt and a scrunch of pepper. Carefully peel the eggs and roll in a little flour to help the sausage mixture stick.

Divide the sausage mixture into 12 roughly equal handfuls. On a work surface, pat each handful into a rough rectangular shape about 1cm/½in thick. Place a quail egg at one end of the rectangle then roll the meat over the egg, tucking in at the sides and end. The fat in the sausage will help it stick. Roll it around in your hand to even it out and repeat with the other eggs. Chill for at least 30 minutes.

Line up three bowls: one containing the flour, one with the beaten eggs and one with the breadcrumbs. One at a time, roll the sausage-coated eggs in the flour, then in the eggs, then coat in breadcrumbs. Cover and chill until ready to cook.

10–15 MINUTES BEFORE SERVING:

In a large pan, heat the oil to 170°C/340°F, or until a cube of bread sizzles and turns golden in 30 seconds. Carefully drop the eggs into the hot oil, 6 at a time. Cook for 4–5 minutes, turning occasionally if necessary, until crisp and golden. Transfer to a plate lined with kitchen paper and keep them warm while you cook the rest. Serve with brown sauce.

TART: Sprinkle a little smoked salt on the eggs before serving.

TWEAK: You can buy ready-peeled quail eggs, although they lack the wibbly-wobbly yolk.

ARANCINI EGGS

MAKES 12

12 quail eggs
a knob of butter
1 shallot, peeled and
    finely chopped
1 garlic clove, peeled and
    finely chopped
200g/7oz/1 cup Arborio
    risotto rice
150ml/5fl oz/⅔ cup dry
    white wine
750ml/1¼ pints/3 cups hot
    vegetable or chicken stock
50g/1¾oz Parmesan cheese,
    grated
salt and pepper
2 tbsp flour, seasoned with salt
    and pepper
2 eggs, lightly beaten
50g/1¾oz/½ cup fine dried
    breadcrumbs
1 litre/1¾ pints/4 cups
    vegetable oil

TART: Turn this into a
kedgeree Scotch egg: add
2 tsp curry powder to the
shallot at the beginning,
and 50g/1¾oz finely flaked,
cooked smoked haddock
and 3 tbsp cream at the end,
omitting the Parmesan.
TWEAK: Instead of a quail
egg, opt for more traditional
arancini, putting a chunk of
mozzarella in the middle.

This is a twist on Scotch eggs (pp.34–36), substituting risotto for the sausage meat to make a sort of vegetarian-friendly arancino-cum-Scotch egg. As with the Scotch eggs, there are several steps, but none are particularly difficult and most of them can be done a day ahead.

A warning, though – I've found that when made with risotto that has been cooked *al dente*, the rice doesn't hold particularly well. So it's not necessarily one for leftovers, unless you cook your risotto to a softer consistency than is strictly authentic.

UP TO A DAY AHEAD:

Fill a bowl with cold water and ice. Bring a pan of water to a boil and carefully drop in 6 of the quail eggs. Boil for 2 minutes, then transfer to the iced water and set aside while you boil the remaining eggs.

Melt the butter in a saucepan over a medium-low heat and cook the shallot and garlic for about 10 minutes, until softened. Whack up the heat and add the rice. Stir for a minute or two, then add the wine and simmer until almost entirely reduced. Add a ladle of stock and continue to simmer, stirring regularly and adding a ladle of stock whenever the rice looks dry. Cook for about 25 minutes, or until the rice is soft and what you might ordinarily consider overcooked. Stir in the Parmesan, season with salt and pepper to taste and leave to cool.

Carefully peel the quail eggs and roll in a little flour to help the rice cling to the eggs. Take a handful of rice and pat it flat in your palm. Lay an egg in the middle and shape the rice around the outside, gently rolling it between your palms to firm. Repeat with the remaining eggs and chill for 30 minutes.

Line up three bowls, the first containing the flour, the second the beaten eggs, and the third the breadcrumbs. One at a time, coat the risotto balls in flour – shaking off any excess – then in egg, and finally in the breadcrumbs. Cover and chill until ready to cook.

10–15 MINUTES BEFORE SERVING:

In a large pan, heat the oil to about 170°C/340°F, or until a cube of bread sizzles and turns golden in 30 seconds. Carefully drop in the risotto balls, 6 at a time, and fry for 4–5 minutes, until golden. Transfer to a plate lined with kitchen paper and keep them warm while you cook the rest, then serve.

VENISON RISSOLES

MAKES 12

200g/7oz venison, minced (ground) in a blender or finely chopped

100g/3½oz pork sausage meat

1 red chilli, deseeded and finely chopped

1 tsp thyme leaves, finely chopped

70g/2½oz/¾ cup fine dried breadcrumbs

salt and pepper

1 tbsp flour

paprika

1 egg

500ml/18fl oz/generous 2 cups vegetable oil

A rissole is essentially a deep-fried meatball. They are a particularly good thing to make with leftover meat – Christmas turkey being a favourite of mine – though you can just as happily cook them with raw ingredients. If you can't find venison, use lamb mince. Having prepared the rissoles the day before your dinner, they just need a quick dip in hot oil before you bring them, piping hot, to the table. Serve with mustard, or a good sweet chilli sauce such as Lingham's.

UP TO A DAY AHEAD:

In a bowl, combine the venison mince, sausage meat, chilli, thyme and a small handful of the breadcrumbs, and season with salt and pepper. Don't overmix or the texture will suffer. Form into 12 balls and chill for 30 minutes.

Season the flour with salt, pepper and paprika, and put it in a bowl. Beat the egg and put it in another bowl. Put the remaining breadcrumbs in a third bowl. One at a time, toss the rissoles in flour, then in the beaten egg, then coat in breadcrumbs. Cover and chill until ready to cook.

10–15 MINUTES BEFORE SERVING:

In a large pan, heat the oil to 170°C/340°F, or until a cube of bread sizzles and turns golden in 30 seconds. Carefully drop the rissoles into the hot oil, in batches if necessary, and cook for 4–5 minutes, until crisp and golden. Drain on kitchen paper, season with a pinch of sea salt, and serve.

TART: Rissoles are traditionally rather more lavishly spiced, originally to disguise the fact that they were made from meat that had been hanging around too long, so spice them with the likes of cumin, coriander seeds, cinnamon and clove.

TWEAK: If you prefer not to deep-fry, drizzle the uncooked rissoles with a little oil and bake at 220°C/425°F/Gas mark 7 for 10 minutes.

CHEESE AND HAM CROQUETTES

SERVES 6–8

1 large floury potato, such as
    King Edward or Maris Piper
50g/1¾oz cooked ham,
    finely chopped
1 tbsp crème fraîche
50g/1¾oz Cheddar cheese,
    grated
25g/1oz Parmesan cheese,
    grated

a small handful of chives,
    finely chopped
salt and pepper
2 tbsp flour, seasoned with
    salt and pepper
1 egg, beaten
50g/1¾oz/½ cup fine dried
    breadcrumbs
500ml/18fl oz/generous 2 cups
    vegetable oil

These oozy fellows are a great way of using leftover mashed potato, though it's more than worth knocking them up from scratch. Either way, they're a shining example of do-ahead dining, as they absolutely *must* find their way to a fridge, both before and ideally after shaping.

UP TO A DAY AHEAD:

Peel and chop the potato and boil in salted water for 15–20 minutes, until soft. Drain and leave to steam for a minute or two – this gets rid of excess moisture – then mash good and proper.

Stir the ham, crème fraîche, cheeses and chives through the mash and season with a pinch of salt and a few twists of pepper. Cool, cover and chill for at least 1 hour.

Once chilled and firm, form into balls or sausages and, one at a time, roll first in seasoned flour, then in beaten egg, then coat thoroughly in the breadcrumbs. Cover and chill.

15 MINUTES BEFORE SERVING:

In a large pan, heat the oil to 170°C/340°F, or until a cube of bread sizzles and turns golden in 30 seconds. Carefully add the croquettes, a few at a time, and cook for 4–5 minutes, until crisp and golden. Drain on kitchen paper and serve with a smear of English mustard.

TART: A little truffle would be a great treat here – try adding a hefty pinch of truffle salt to the potato.
TWEAK: Instead of the ham, crème fraîche and cheeses, beat some of the brandade on p.44 into the mashed potato, for salt cod (pollack) croquettes.

Things on toast

Most things go well on toast. In fact, I'd go so far as to say that if you want to get a fussy eater to try something, stick it on a piece of grilled, oiled and garlicked bread. I once tricked a friend into eating duck hearts this way, and she loved 'em. At least until I told her what they were. There's nothing quite so voodoo as that here – just good, homely stuff.

WELSH RABBIT

SERVES 6

25g/1oz/2 tbsp butter
25g/1oz/3 tbsp flour
150ml/5fl oz/⅔ cup ale
300g/10½oz mature Cheddar
   cheese, grated
1 tbsp English mustard
Worcestershire sauce
6 slices of bread, halved
pepper

This dish originated from the notion that the Welsh are not the most generous of hosts, and so should a Welshman invite you round for something delicious like rabbit, you'd more likely be fed cheese on toast. Not a bad trade-off in my book. Which is why it's in my book.

It may surprise you to know that this can be made several hours in advance, and needs only 2–3 minutes under the grill at the last minute.

UP TO 6 HOURS AHEAD:

Melt the butter in a saucepan over a medium heat. Add the flour and simmer for a minute or two, stirring continuously, then add the beer. Simmer for a further 2 minutes, stirring until smooth and glossy. Turn the heat to low and add a handful of the cheese. Stir until melted, then continue adding handfuls of cheese, stirring until thick and smooth. Take off the heat and add the mustard and a few shakes of Worcestershire sauce. Taste for seasoning and add a little pepper if necessary. Cool for 10 minutes.

Meanwhile, lightly toast the bread and leave to cool for 10 minutes or so. Put the toast on a baking sheet and top with the cheese mixture. Cover and chill.

DINNERTIME:

Preheat the grill to high. Grill the rabbits for 2–3 minutes until brown and bubbly, and serve.

TART: At the Thatched House pub in Hammersmith, west London, they serve this with crisp streaky bacon on top.
TWEAK: If you can find some, try using smoked porter instead of ale.

CHICKEN LIVERS AND CELERIAC REMOULADE

SERVES 6

olive oil

1 shallot, peeled and
    finely chopped

salt and pepper

50g/1¾oz/4 tbsp butter

300g/10½oz chicken livers,
    trimmed of any green bits
    and roughly chopped

1 tsp finely chopped thyme

2 tbsp sherry or red wine
    vinegar

6 slices of bread, halved

For the celeriac remoulade

1 small celeriac, about
    400g/14oz

4 tbsp mayonnaise
    (good shop-bought
    or homemade)

1 tbsp grainy mustard

juice of 1 lemon

There will, celeriac being the size they are, be leftovers of the remoulade. However, it will keep for a good few days in the fridge, and is delicious tossed through a salad, served alongside a terrine, or even just eaten on buttered toast. Or you could forget the remoulade and serve the chicken livers on toast with a dollop of chutney.

UP TO A DAY AHEAD:

Heat a few drops of oil in a frying pan over a low heat and add the shallot. Season with salt and pepper and cook until softened, stirring occasionally. Whack up the heat and add the butter, livers, thyme and vinegar, stirring regularly for 4–5 minutes, until the livers are cooked. Mash with a wooden spoon until you have a coarse pâté, and set aside to cool. Cover and chill until needed.

To make the celeriac remoulade, peel and quarter the celeriac, then grate on the medium-thin setting – between grated cheese and lemon zest. Stir in the mayonnaise, mustard and lemon juice and taste for seasoning. Chill until needed.

1 HOUR AHEAD:

Get the livers and celeriac out of the fridge.

DINNERTIME:

Toast the bread, spread with butter and top with the livers, then the celeriac. Drizzle with a little olive oil and serve.

TART: For a more refined, if less healthy, mouthful, add 100g/3½oz/ 7 tbsp butter to the pan with the livers, cook as above, then blend until smooth.

TWEAK: Instead of the chicken livers, top the toasts with slices of that lovely Italian air-dried beef, bresaola.

TOMORROW: Leftover livers can be added last minute to a Bolognese sauce.

POLLACK
BRANDADE

SERVES 6

200g/7oz fine sea salt
300g/10½oz pollack
100ml/3½fl oz/6 tbsp olive oil
100ml/3½fl oz/6 tbsp whole
    milk
pepper
To serve
6 slices of bread, halved
1 garlic clove, cut in half
olive oil

This rich, salted fish purée is traditionally made using salt cod, but that can be tricky to find, and with cod being a somewhat controversial commodity, it's very straightforward to use the more sustainable – and considerably cheaper – pollack. If you can't find pollack, by all means use cod, but make sure it's sustainably caught.

4 DAYS AHEAD:

Sprinkle a glass or ceramic dish with half of the salt and lay the pollack on top. Cover with the remaining salt, then wrap tightly with clingfilm and refrigerate for 2 days.

2 DAYS AHEAD:

Remove the fish from the dish and rinse off all the excess salt. Wrap in a tea towel and return to the fridge for a day.

1 DAY AHEAD:

Soak the fish overnight in fresh water, changing the water a few times.

UP TO 6 HOURS AHEAD:

Bring a pan of water to a gentle boil and poach the fish for 7 minutes, until flaking. Remove and flake apart, chucking any bones.

Warm the oil over a medium heat and, when hot, add the fish, mashing and stirring until it starts to resemble mashed potato. Add the milk a little at a time, and continue stirring until completely smooth. Nudge it along with a blender if you wish. Season with pepper and set aside.

DINNERTIME:

Preheat the grill to medium-high. Toast the bread, then rub with the cut garlic clove. Top with the brandade and return to the grill for 3 minutes, until lightly browned. Drizzle with olive oil and serve.

TART: Blend marinated red peppers with parsley and a little olive oil and drizzle over the toasts. Resist making jokes about American abstract artists.

TWEAK: You can use shop-bought salt cod; you will need to soak it for 24 hours to soften it thoroughly. Find it in Italian, Spanish and Caribbean stores.

PEA, WATERCRESS AND MUSTARD

SERVES 6
300g/10½oz/2 cups frozen
    peas
100g/3½oz watercress
25g/1oz/2 tbsp butter
1 tbsp grainy mustard
salt and pepper
To serve
6 slices of bread, halved
1 garlic clove, cut in half
olive oil

This topping works both hot and cold, though served hot it's not so do-ahead. Up to you.

UP TO A DAY AHEAD:
Bring a pan of salted water to a boil and add the peas. Simmer for 3 minutes then drain. Roughly mash with the watercress, butter and mustard, and season with salt and pepper. Or blend for a smoother texture. Cover and chill, or continue to dinnertime.

30 MINUTES AHEAD (IF NECESSARY):
Take the pea purée out of the fridge.

DINNERTIME:
Toast the bread, then rub with the cut garlic clove and drizzle with a little oil. Top the toasts with the pea and watercress purée, finish with a little more olive oil and a scrunch of pepper, and serve.

TART: A sliver of smoked chicken on top would meat this up.
TWEAK: Replace the mustard with a good handful of freshly grated Parmesan cheese.

Soups

Soup is do-ahead cooking at its most pure and simple. There is barely a broth, bouillon or bisque that won't improve by being made some time in advance, no velouté that won't benefit from having a good few hours to let the flavours commingle. Nor are there many things more soothing and heartening with which to begin a meal – whether a cooling cucumber and yogurt soup at the end of a stinking hot day, or a belly-warming consommé on a crisp December evening, soup has an extraordinary ability to cheer a flagging spirit.

It's a crowd-pleaser, too. Unless you happen to have a friend who loathes, say, courgettes above all other things, you're pretty safe with soup. It's comforting and atavistic and unchallenging. Not that it has to be boring. I wouldn't turn my nose up at any brew, but it's nice to add a little bit of character to what can occasionally be a pedestrian dish.

Portion sizes err on the modest, considering soup's context within this book as a starter, so keep this in mind if you're cooking these recipes as a main meal. A few more vegetables here, a little more stock there, and these bulk up very easily.

CELERIAC SOUP WITH CRISPY SHALLOTS

SERVES 4–6

25g/1oz/2 tbsp butter

8 tbsp olive oil

1 onion, peeled and finely chopped

1 garlic clove, peeled and sliced

salt and pepper

1 large celeriac, about 750g/1lb 10oz, peeled and chopped into chunks

1 litre/1¾ pints/4 cups chicken or vegetable stock

200ml/7fl oz/generous ¾ cup double (heavy) cream

300g/10½oz shallots, peeled and finely sliced

2 tsp finely chopped thyme leaves

I often think soups are best when they have some added element of excitement. After three mouthfuls of straight-up blended vegetable it starts to become a bit of a slog, there being no variation in texture or flavour, and it's not long before you feel like you're eating a bowl of baby food. Here, a tangle of crunchy, herby shallots adds another dimension.

UP TO A DAY AHEAD:

Melt the butter in a large pan with 2 tbsp of the oil, then add the onion and garlic. Season with salt and pepper, cover, and cook over a low heat for 10–15 minutes, until totally softened. Add the celeriac and the stock and bring to a boil. Simmer uncovered for 20–25 minutes, until the celeriac is cooked through. Blend until smooth. Leave to cool, cover and chill.

30 MINUTES AHEAD:

Gently reheat the soup over a low heat, stirring occasionally. Don't boil.

10 MINUTES AHEAD:

Check the soup for seasoning and stir in the cream.

Put the remaining oil in a frying pan over a medium-high heat and throw in the shallots. Cook, stirring regularly, until crisp, then remove to kitchen paper using a slotted spoon. Sprinkle with the thyme.

DINNERTIME:

Ladle the soup into bowls and top with a handful of crispy shallots. Finish with a pinch of salt and a drizzle of olive oil.

TART: Blend a small bunch of parsley with a pinch of ground cumin, a squeeze of lemon juice and a glug of olive oil, and drizzle over the soup before serving.

TWEAK: Beetroot would work well here instead of celeriac, or try half beetroot, half celeriac.

TOMORROW: Store in the fridge for a couple of days, or freeze.

PRAWN GUMBO

SERVES 4–6

50g/1¾oz/4 tbsp butter
50g/1¾oz/7 tbsp plain (all-
    purpose) flour
1 onion, peeled and
    finely chopped
2 sticks of celery,
    finely chopped
2 garlic cloves, peeled and
    crushed to a paste
1 green pepper, deseeded
    and finely chopped
1 tsp cayenne pepper
salt and pepper
2 large tomatoes,
    finely chopped
500ml/18fl oz/generous 2 cups
    fish stock
400g/14oz raw prawns
    (shrimp)
2 spring onions (scallions),
    finely sliced at an angle
lemon wedges, to serve

There's a fair amount of jostling concerning the etymology of 'gumbo', a traditional Louisiana soup, though it seems most likely that it derives from a West African word for okra. There's no okra in this recipe, you may notice. Add some if you like.

UP TO A DAY AHEAD:

Melt the butter in a large saucepan over a medium heat, add the flour and cook for about 5 minutes, stirring regularly to avoid burning, until caramel coloured. Add the onion, celery, garlic, green pepper and cayenne, and season with salt and pepper. Cook for another 10 minutes, stirring regularly.

Add the tomatoes and fish stock, and bring to a gentle boil. Simmer for 10 minutes, then cool, cover and chill, or continue, skipping the next step.

15 MINUTES AHEAD:

Bring the gumbo back to a gentle boil.

5 MINUTES AHEAD:

Add the prawns and simmer for 5 minutes.

DINNERTIME:

Ladle the gumbo into bowls and serve with a scattering of spring onions and a wedge of lemon.

TART: Add a good handful of sliced okra to the gumbo along with the prawns.
TWEAK: For a lighter gumbo, omit the flour and butter, and simply fry the vegetables in a little oil.
TOMORROW: Leftover gumbo is delicious served with rice.

BORSCHT

SERVES 4–6

500g/1lb 2oz beetroot
olive oil
1 onion, peeled and
    finely chopped
2 sticks of celery,
    finely chopped
1 garlic clove, peeled and
    finely chopped
salt and pepper
500ml/18fl oz/generous 2 cups
    chicken or vegetable stock
1 tbsp white wine vinegar or
    tarragon vinegar
To serve
a small bunch of chives or dill
sour cream

We've done a couple of raucous Soviet-themed evenings at the Secret Larder, invoking the revolutionary spirit, chucking back pickled fish and chilled vodka, and generally behaving like Cossacks. It's a fun cuisine to play around with. The cooking is simple but more delicious than you might expect, and cheap (unless you're an oligarch with a taste for caviar), leaving you with some wedge to buy a bottle of half-decent vodka. Russian Standard is good, and easy to find, though it's worth rootling out Chase, which is made from British spuds.

Serve the borscht – a Ukrainian dish, originally – hot or chilled with a glass of iced vodka. If serving chilled, allow at least 6 hours for it to get thoroughly cold.

UP TO A DAY AHEAD:

Put the beetroot in a pan of salted water and bring to a boil. Gently simmer until easily pierced with a skewer – this can take anything from 20 minutes to 1 hour, depending on their size and age. Drain and cool for a few minutes, then rub with your thumb to remove the skin. Chop into 2cm/¾in dice and set aside.

Meanwhile, heat a little oil in a large saucepan over a low heat and gently sweat the onion, celery and garlic until softened. Season with salt and pepper, and add the stock, vinegar and cooked beetroot. Bring to a boil and simmer for 5 minutes. Taste for seasoning, then cool and chill.

30 MINUTES AHEAD:

Gently reheat the soup if serving hot. Chop the chives or dill.

DINNERTIME:

Spoon the borscht into bowls and garnish with sour cream and chopped herbs.

TART: A few flakes of smoked mackerel would certainly go well, as would shredded cabbage or apple added with the beetroot, though I enjoy the simplicity of the dish.
TWEAK: Once the soup is cooked, blend with a splash of cream for a more refined, if less authentic, borscht.
TOMORROW: Store in the fridge for a couple of days.

VICHYSSOISE

SERVES 4–6

20g/¾oz/1½ tbsp butter
1 onion, peeled and
 finely chopped
500g/1lb 2oz leeks, white bits
 only, chopped
salt and pepper
300g/10½oz floury potatoes,
 such as Maris Piper or
 King Edward
900ml/generous 1½ pints/
 3½ cups chicken stock or
 vegetable stock
150ml/5fl oz/⅔ cup double
 (heavy) cream
a small bunch of chives

Another 'classic' dish over whose origins there's a fair amount of wrangling. A chef in New York historically claims ownership – with Julia Child backing him up – though it seems unlikely that a Frenchman hadn't considered putting potatoes and leeks in a soup before the early twentieth century. One of the great mysteries of life. Vichyssoise is traditionally served chilled, and as such you'll need to make it at least 6 hours ahead; some like it hot (and why not?), though it's really then just leek and potato soup.

I'd hesitantly suggest that the key here is really good chicken stock, though of course vegetable stock will produce something delicious, too, should you be entertaining a non-meat-eater.

UP TO A DAY AHEAD (THOUGH NO FEWER THAN 6 HOURS):
Melt the butter in a large saucepan and add the onions and leeks, with a pinch of salt and pepper. Cover and cook over a low heat for 10–15 minutes, until softened. Meanwhile, peel and dice the potatoes. Add them to the pan with the stock and bring to a boil. Simmer for 15–20 minutes, until the potatoes are cooked through. Add the cream and blend thoroughly. Taste for seasoning and leave to cool, then chill.

30 MINUTES AHEAD:
Finely chop the chives.

DINNERTIME:
Give the vichyssoise a stir and check again for seasoning: you may find it needs a pinch of salt. Serve in bowls with a sprinkling of chives.

TART: For a knockout touch, freeze chive flowers in ice cubes and serve in the vichyssoise.
TWEAK: The soup can also be served hot, either immediately after cooking or reheated before dinner.
TOMORROW: Vichyssoise will keep in the fridge for a couple of days, and freezes well.

PAPPA AL POMODORO

SERVES 4–6

olive oil

1 onion, peeled and
    finely chopped

2 garlic cloves, peeled and
    finely chopped

1kg/2¼lb tomatoes,
    roughly chopped

2 tbsp white wine vinegar

2 tsp sugar

salt and pepper

2–3 chunks of stale bread

a handful of basil leaves

a handful of grated Parmesan
    cheese (optional)

I'm afraid I'm going to have to break a promise to myself here. I vowed that I'd leave it to you to decide which ingredients you buy – organic or not, local or not, etc. – but it would be remiss of me not to emphasize the fact that this dish relies entirely on the quality of what goes in it. Being a simple tomato and bread soup, it will not work if you use anaemic January toms and a couple of slices of Mighty White. You need the best, ripest tomatoes you can find and good, but slightly stale, bread – ideally sourdough, though it would also be delicious with ciabatta (p.11).

UP TO 3 DAYS AHEAD:

Heat a little oil in a large pan over a low heat, add the onion and garlic and cook until softened, stirring regularly. Add the tomatoes, vinegar, sugar and a good slosh of water. Season with salt and pepper, cover and cook for 40 minutes over a medium-low heat, until the tomatoes are cooked.

Tear the bread and add to the soup, along with the basil. Simmer, uncovered, for another 5 minutes. If it's a little thick, then add another splash of water. Check for seasoning, cool and chill.

30 MINUTES AHEAD:

If necessary, gently reheat the soup.

DINNERTIME:

Serve the pappa al pomodoro garnished with torn basil, a drizzle of olive oil and grated Parmesan if you fancy it.

TART: Pep up the soup with a pinch of dried chilli flakes along with the onion, or you could try stirring in some chorizo or 'nduja, a spicy salami from Calabria.

TWEAK: Halve the tomatoes and roast with olive oil, garlic and fresh oregano at 220°C/425°F/Gas mark 7 for a toasty flavour.

TOMORROW: This will keep for a good few days in the fridge.

PEA AND COURGETTE SOUP WITH YOGURT AND HARISSA

SERVES 4–6

olive oil

1 onion, peeled and
    finely chopped

1 garlic clove, peeled and
    finely sliced

salt and pepper

1 medium potato, peeled
    and diced

750ml/1¼ pints/3 cups
    chicken or vegetable stock

400g/14oz courgettes
    (zucchini), washed
    and chopped

400g/14oz frozen peas

a bunch of parsley, leaves
    and stalks separated

juice of ½ lemon

To serve

thick plain yogurt

harissa

I love the North African chilli paste, harissa. Its combination of heat and smoke and sweetness and bite makes it an asset to almost any savoury dish, be it served alongside grilled fish or stirred through mayonnaise and stuck in a sandwich. Try to find harissa that includes rose, which adds an intoxicating, floral edge.

This soup is excellent chilled, the harissa providing its little burst of heat. If you want to serve it chilled, it will need at least 6 hours in the fridge.

UP TO A DAY AHEAD:

Heat a little oil in a saucepan over a low heat and add the onion and garlic. Season with salt and pepper, cover and cook for 10–15 minutes, until softened. Add the potato and stock, and bring to a boil. Add the courgettes and simmer for 5–7 minutes, until the potato is cooked. Add the peas and parsley stalks and simmer for 2 minutes, then add the parsley leaves and simmer for a further minute. Blend until smooth. Add the lemon juice and taste for seasoning. Cool and chill.

30 MINUTES AHEAD:

If necessary, gently reheat the soup.

DINNERTIME:

Check the seasoning, then ladle into bowls and top with a dollop of yogurt and a few flicks of harissa.

TART: Zhoosh up the yogurt with chopped mint, a little crushed garlic and grated cucumber – especially good if you're serving the soup chilled.

TWEAK: Considering the colours of the soup, you could go for an Italian angle here, replacing the harissa with *olio, aglio e peperoncino* sauce (the stuff based on sun-dried tomatoes – you can buy this in an Italian deli or in some supermarkets) and adding chunks of mozzarella or burrata instead of the yogurt.

TOMORROW: Store in the fridge for a couple of days, or freeze.

FENNEL SOUP WITH BROWN SHRIMP AND DILL

SERVES 4–6

25g/1oz/2 tbsp butter

2 shallots, peeled and chopped

1 stick of celery, trimmed and finely chopped

1 tsp fennel seeds, crushed

1 medium potato, peeled and diced

2 fennel bulbs (about 500g/1lb 2oz total), trimmed and chopped

900ml/generous 1½ pints/ 3½ cups vegetable, chicken, or fish stock

salt and pepper

100g/3½oz small brown shrimps

a small bunch of dill

olive oil

Here we have a double whammy of anise, with its sweet soft spice being provided by both the fennel and its seeds. Serving this with a glass of pastis might be over-egging it somewhat, though I would enthusiastically recommend it as an accompaniment to the cooking process.

This makes a fresh-tasting chilled soup, for which you'll need to allow at least 6 hours in the fridge, although you can serve hot.

UP TO A DAY AHEAD (THOUGH NO FEWER THAN 6 HOURS):

Melt the butter in a large pan over a low heat and add the shallots and celery. Season with salt and pepper, cover and cook for 15 minutes until softened, stirring occasionally. Add the crushed fennel seeds, potato, fennel and stock. Bring to a boil and simmer for 10 minutes, until the fennel is cooked, then blend until smooth. Taste for seasoning, leave to cool, cover and chill.

30 MINUTES AHEAD (IF SERVING HOT):

If necessary, gently reheat the soup.

DINNERTIME:

Ladle the soup into bowls and garnish with brown shrimps, sprigs of dill and a drizzle of olive oil.

TART: Finely chop a small fennel bulb and cook in butter over a medium heat for about 15 minutes until caramelized. Garnish the soup with the fennel.

TOMORROW: Store the soup in the fridge for a couple of days, or freeze. Any extra brown shrimps can be tossed through a salad or prodded into a sandwich.

A SMOKY SWEETCORN SOUP

SERVES 4–6

1 chipotle chilli
olive oil
1 red onion, peeled and
    finely chopped
2 garlic cloves, peeled and
    finely sliced
4 corn cobs, or 500g/1lb 2oz
    canned sweetcorn
1 tsp ground cumin
1 tsp ground coriander
salt and pepper
650ml/generous 1 pint/
    2¾ cups chicken or
    vegetable stock
juice of 1 lime
To serve
a bunch of coriander
    (cilantro)
sour cream

The smokiness of this Aztec-style soup comes from the chipotle – a smoked and dried jalapeño chilli. They're no more difficult to track down than a CD, in that you can buy them very easily online, and they are becoming increasingly available in the shops, too. Unlike CDs. They will transform a chilli con carne, adding a rich, smoky fruit that delivers a surprising punch at the end, and are a very handy thing to have on standby for Empty Fridge Nights. You *could* use normal dried chillies and a pinch of smoked paprika, but it's worth the effort to find the chipotles.

UP TO 2 DAYS AHEAD:

Pour boiling water over the chipotle and leave to soak for 10 minutes, then finely chop. Heat a little oil in a large saucepan over a low heat, add the onion and garlic, and cook gently until softened. Meanwhile, remove the husks from the corn cobs, if using, and rub off any hairy bits. Stand the cobs upright on a chopping board. Using a sharp knife, slice down the sides to cut the kernels away. Add them to the pan, along with the chilli and spices, season with salt and pepper and add the stock. Bring to a boil and simmer for 7 minutes, until the corn is tender. Roughly blend or, if you prefer, blend until smooth and pass through a sieve. Add the lime juice and taste for seasoning. Cool, cover and chill until needed.

30 MINUTES AHEAD:

If necessary, gently reheat the soup. Pick the leaves from the coriander.

DINNERTIME:

Ladle the soup into bowls and garnish with a dollop of sour cream and a few coriander leaves.

TART: For a more substantial, main-course-style dish, stir some shredded slow-cooked beef, or chicken, through the soup.
TWEAK: Transform this from a soup into a zippy side dish for a barbecue by draining the cooked corn before blending.
TOMORROW: The soup will keep for a few days in the fridge.

A HOT AND SOUR BROTH

SERVES 4–6

1 tsp fennel seeds
½ tsp Szechwan peppercorns
1 clove
2 star anise
2 cinnamon sticks
1 small thumb of fresh ginger,
   peeled and cut into
   matchsticks
1 garlic clove, peeled and
   finely sliced
2 shallots, peeled and sliced
2 birdseye (Thai) chillies,
   finely sliced
1 tbsp Thai fish sauce
2 tbsp soy sauce
2 tbsp Shaoxing rice wine
a few shakes of sesame oil
1.2 litres/2 pints/5 cups water
4 chicken thighs
4 spring onions (scallions)
a bunch of coriander
   (cilantro)
lime wedges, to serve

I use the base of this soup as a springboard for lunch on an almost weekly basis. It's simple, quick, healthy, and amazingly aromatic and evocative. What you choose to bulk it up with is largely up to you. I have used chicken here, but almost anything goes – prawns, pak choi, noodles – and even without any meat or veg it's a remarkably restorative concoction.

UP TO A DAY AHEAD:

Crush the fennel seeds, Szechwan peppercorns and clove in a pestle and mortar. Put all the ingredients except the chicken, spring onions and coriander in a pan and bring to a boil. Reduce the heat and simmer for 15 minutes, then add the chicken. Gently poach for 1 hour, then remove the chicken using a slotted spoon and set aside for 10 minutes. Discard the skin and bone, shred the meat and return it to the pan. Cool, cover and chill until needed.

30 MINUTES AHEAD:

Gently reheat the broth if necessary. Trim the spring onions, then finely slice at an angle. Pick the leaves from the coriander.

DINNERTIME:

Ladle the soup into bowls and garnish with spring onions and coriander leaves. Serve with a wedge of lime.

TART: For a more substantial, midweek supper kind of dish, add some green vegetables such as pak choi towards the end of cooking, and serve spooned over cooked rice noodles.

TWEAK: For a clearer broth, strain the liquid after taking out the cooked chicken in order to get rid of the spices and onion. Then shred the chicken and return to the broth.

TOMORROW: Store in the fridge for a couple of days. Eat leftovers for lunch with noodles or rice.

JERUSALEM ARTICHOKE SOUP WITH ROAST ONION, MUSHROOMS AND CHIVES

SERVES 4–6

20g/¾oz/1½ tbsp butter
1 onion, peeled and
    finely chopped
salt and pepper
500g/1lb 2oz Jerusalem
    artichokes
1 medium potato, peeled
    and diced
750ml/1¼ pints/3 cups
    chicken or vegetable stock
For the roast onion
1 red onion
olive oil
a sprig of thyme, leaves only
For the mushrooms
25g/1oz/2 tbsp butter
1 garlic clove, peeled and
    finely chopped
100g/3½oz mushrooms
    – chestnut (cremini)
    or shiitake work well –
    quartered
a small bunch of parsley,
    finely chopped
To finish
a small bunch of chives

Jerusalem artichokes have a reputation for causing some, ahem, adverse side effects, and indeed the midnight fanfare these little tubers can conduct may put you off ever eating them. In my view, they are delicious and worth the potential discomfort; furthermore, I find that when cooked like this, they're not quite so vocal.

UP TO A DAY AHEAD:

To make the roast onion, preheat the oven to 180°C/350°F/ Gas mark 4. Cut the red onion into wedges (4 or 6 pieces, depending on how many servings) and toss with salt, pepper, olive oil and thyme leaves in a small baking dish. Roast in the oven for 30–35 minutes, then cover and chill.

Meanwhile, melt the butter in a large pan and add the chopped onion. Season with salt and pepper, cover and cook over a low heat until soft. Peel the Jerusalem artichokes and chop into even-sized pieces – don't do this too far ahead or they'll discolour. Keep in water with a little lemon juice or vinegar in it if you need to delay cooking.

Add the potato, artichokes and stock to the pan, bring to a boil and simmer for 15–20 minutes. Blend until smooth. Check for seasoning, leave to cool, then cover and chill until needed.

30 MINUTES AHEAD:

Reheat the soup over a low heat, stirring occasionally. Warm the roast onion through in the oven. Finely chop the chives.

For the mushrooms, melt the butter in a frying pan and add the garlic, stirring to avoid burning, then toss in the mushrooms and parsley. Season with salt and pepper and cook over a medium heat, stirring occasionally, until softened.

DINNERTIME:

Ladle the soup into bowls, adding a piece of roast onion and a few mushrooms to each bowl. Finish with chives and a drizzle of olive oil.

TART: My friend Tom kindly gave me a little pot of truffle salt for my birthday, which finishes a dish like this off brilliantly. It's not cheap – or the good stuff isn't – but a little goes a very long way.
TWEAK: If you're not keen on Jerusalem artichokes for whatever reasons, use the same amount of cauliflower instead.
TOMORROW: Store the soup in the fridge for a couple of days, or freeze. Roast an extra 1 or 2 onions to add to salads, and any leftover mushrooms can find their way into a pasta sauce or a risotto.

Starters

I remember one of the teachers at Ballymaloe Cookery School explaining that for a chef the starter is the most important part of a menu. Get it right and your punters are likely to spend a good deal of money; get it wrong and they'll be out the door before the pudding menu arrives. Of course, the same doesn't go for the home, where your guests have to stay put whether they like it or not, but it's a good thing to keep in mind. It is a meal's 'curtain up', the opening sequence that sets the pace and mood, as well as the moment when your guests decide, subconsciously or otherwise, how good the next couple of hours' eating are going to be.

If this sounds alarming, it's not supposed to, for the best thing about starters is the simple punch with which they can be delivered. You don't, on the whole, need to worry about side dishes and sauces, or about one flavour muting the others. A starter is the springboard into a meal, and you can make it as pithy as you wish.

In terms of do-aheadability, starters can for the most part be ready by the time your guests arrive. Based on conversations with various friends, the thing that most alarms them about cooking a 'dinner party' is the idea of having a hundred things to do in the kitchen when they want to be with their guests. Having the starter done well in advance means there's at least one hefty aspect of the meal that you don't have to think about come seven o'clock.

BURNT CHICORY, PICKLED PEAR, GORGONZOLA AND CARAMELIZED WALNUTS

SERVES 4–6

For the pickled pears
500ml/18fl oz/generous 2 cups white wine vinegar
300g/10½oz/1½ cups caster (superfine) sugar
1 cinnamon stick
1 star anise
1 clove
3 under-ripe pears

For the caramelized walnuts
50g/1¾oz/¼ cup sugar
50g/1¾oz/6 tbsp walnut pieces
1 tsp smoked salt (or normal salt)

To assemble
about 85g/3oz Gorgonzola cheese
1 tbsp white wine vinegar or tarragon vinegar
3 tbsp olive oil
salt and pepper
2–3 heads of chicory (half per person)

This is all about the combination of sweet and sour, salt and bitterness. It's pretty straightforward and all the key components can be prepared in advance, but it's an absolute knockout. The pickled pears make a lovely Christmas present, so I thoroughly recommend making double.

UP TO A YEAR AHEAD:

To make the pickled pears, put the vinegar, sugar and spices in a large saucepan and bring to a boil, stirring until the sugar has dissolved. Peel the pears and drop into the water, then simmer gently for 45 minutes, turning occasionally. Store in sterilized jars (see note on p.2) along with the pickling juice and spices.

UP TO A WEEK AHEAD:

To make the caramelized walnuts, start by rubbing a baking sheet with a little oil. Put the sugar in a frying pan over a medium heat and melt, shaking occasionally to redistribute the sugar, but not stirring. Once melted, continue cooking until the caramel is a dark whisky colour. Add the nuts and salt and swirl to coat thoroughly, then tip the walnuts onto the oiled baking sheet and leave to cool completely. Break up any large walnut pieces with a rolling pin or roughly chop them, and store in an airtight container.

UP TO A DAY AHEAD:

Crumble the Gorgonzola, cover and chill. Mix the vinegar and oil with a little salt and pepper, bung in a jar and into the fridge.

Halve the chicory and rub the cut sides with olive oil. Get a griddle pan smoking hot and cook the chicory, cut side down, until nicely coloured and a little softened. Cool, cover and chill.

30 MINUTES AHEAD:

Take the chicory, cheese and dressing out of the fridge. Cut the pickled pears into wedges.

DINNERTIME:

Put a piece of chicory on each plate, along with a piece of pear. Scatter the cheese and caramelized walnuts over the top and finish with the dressing.

TWEAK: For a less involved version, use slices of fresh ripe pear and chopped walnuts.

TOMORROW: Use any remaining walnuts and Gorgonzola in the farro risotto (p.80). Pickled pears go very well with other cheeses.

GREEN BEANS, ANCHOVY, QUAIL EGG AND MUSTARD

SERVES 4–6

250g/9oz green beans
salt and pepper
8–12 quail eggs
1 tsp Dijon mustard
the smallest garlic clove
    you can find, crushed
    to a paste
2 tsp white wine vinegar
4 tsp olive oil
12 anchovy fillets

TART: Being only a hop, skip and a jump from a *salade Niçoise*, this could be bulked up with black olives, cherry tomatoes and croutons.
TWEAK: Use asparagus spears instead of green beans.
TOMORROW: Use extra quail eggs to make Scotch eggs (p.34) or arancini eggs (p.38).

A simple and summery salad – a sort of pared-down *salade Niçoise*. It's good as a starter, or with crusty bread and a hunk of cheese as a lunch for two.

Getting the quail eggs done ahead is a major time-saver: with these cooked and peeled, and the beans blanched and chilled, it's a simple matter of putting things on a plate.

UP TO A DAY AHEAD:
Trim the woody bits from the green beans. I don't bother to trim the other end because I think they look nice, but by all means do if you prefer. Bring a pan of salted water to a boil and drop in the beans. Bring back to a boil and simmer for 90 seconds, then drain and transfer to a bowl of iced water to hold their colour and stop them overcooking. When they are cold, drain, cover and chill.

Bring another pan of water to a boil and carefully drop in the quail eggs. Simmer for 2 minutes, then transfer to a bowl of iced water. Leave until cool, then drain and peel. Cover and chill.

Mix the mustard, garlic, vinegar and oil, season with salt and pepper, cover and chill.

1 HOUR AHEAD:
Take all the components out of the fridge.

DINNERTIME:
Put a pile of beans on each serving plate and top with a couple of anchovies. Cut the eggs in half and place on top, then finish with the dressing.

SALAD OF PIG CHEEK WITH RADISH, SHALLOT AND BUTTERMILK

SERVES 6

olive oil
500g/1lb 2oz pig cheeks
salt and pepper
1 litre/1¾ pints/4 cups chicken
   stock
2 shallots
juice of ½ lemon
200g/7oz radishes
100g/3½oz watercress, or
   mixed leaves

For the dressing

2 tsp English mustard
2 tbsp buttermilk
2 tbsp white wine vinegar
3 tbsp olive oil

Pig cheeks are getting much easier to find these days, with at least one supermarket I know of stocking them. That said, it's always good to support independent retailers, and I'm sure your butcher would be more than happy to get some for you. They're a fantastic ingredient – relatively lean, full of flavour, and cheap as chitterlings. They need to cook very gently for 1½ hours, while you can be getting on with other things.

UP TO A DAY AHEAD:

Heat a little oil in a frying pan and brown the pig cheeks on both sides, seasoning with salt and pepper as you go. Bring the stock to a gentle simmer and drop in the pig cheeks. Cook over a low heat for 1½ hours, until very tender. Remove from the stock and cool, then flake apart with a couple of forks or your hands. Cover and chill.

Peel and finely slice the shallots, then mix with the lemon juice, cover and set aside.

Make the dressing: mix the mustard, buttermilk, vinegar and oil, and season with salt and pepper. Cover and chill.

1 HOUR AHEAD:

Finely slice the radishes and leave in a bowl of iced water to help them crisp up. Take the pig cheeks and dressing out of the fridge.

DINNERTIME:

Mix the pig cheeks, salad leaves, radishes, shallots and dressing, and serve.

TART: All manner of tarting would work with this salad, should you want to make it more substantial. Cooked green beans would be a fine addition, as would some crisp croutons. In the spring, wild garlic and chive flowers are colourful and full of flavour.

TWEAK: You can omit the buttermilk if you can't find any; instead, add an extra 1 tbsp olive oil to take the edge off the vinegar.

TOMORROW: Leftover cooked pig cheek can make a spoiling breakfast, tossed through an omelette or alongside a fried egg.

PANZANELLA

SERVES 4–6
a good bunch of basil
1 small garlic clove, peeled
   and crushed to a paste
juice of 1 lemon
125ml/4fl oz/1 cup olive oil
a good handful of
   black olives
2 shallots
1 mozzarella ball, about
   125g/4½oz
4–5 thick slices of stale bread
250ml/9fl oz/generous 1 cup
   whole milk
700g/1lb 9oz ripe tomatoes
2 tbsp olive oil
1 tbsp white wine vinegar
salt, pepper and sugar

This is in many ways an alternative to the *pappa al pomodoro* soup (p.55), being an ingenious Italian means of using up a bit of stale bread and a few ripe tomatoes. Indeed at its most classic and simple, it uses exactly the same ingredients as that wonderful soup, though here it's more of a tricolore salad with makeup on. Purists may not like it, but with any luck your guests will.

It's a very laid-back kind of dish – of course it is, it's Italian – and you can get most of the bits and pieces done ahead. Don't, however, prepare the tomatoes too far in advance, as they'll lose their vitality. And don't for Pete's sake keep tomatoes in the fridge. A cold tomato is an insipid brute.

UP TO 6 HOURS AHEAD:
Put the basil, garlic and lemon juice in a blender and start to blend, pouring in 100ml/3½fl oz/7 tbsp of the oil as you go, until fully blended. Alternatively use a pestle and mortar. Pass though a sieve for a smooth herb oil; otherwise simply cover and set aside.

Pit the olives by squashing them with the flat of a knife and removing the stones. Roughly chop, cover and set aside. Peel the shallots and finely slice them, then set aside.

Tear the mozzarella into smallish pieces, cover and set aside. Cut the bread into chunks and soak in the milk for a minute, then drain and squeeze dry. Cover and store with the rest of the components.

UP TO 1 HOUR AHEAD:
Peel the tomatoes by cutting a cross in their bottoms, putting them in a bowl and covering with boiling water. Leave for a minute, then drain. When cool, the skin should peel off easily. Slice the tomatoes and gently toss in the remaining 2 tbsp of olive oil and the vinegar, along with a good pinch of salt, pepper and sugar.

DINNERTIME:
Lay a few slices of tomato on everyone's plate – or on one big platter for everyone to share – and top with the olives, mozzarella, shallots and bread. Finish with the basil oil and serve.

TART: For a family-style main course, serve with barbecued steaks or chicken and some new potatoes.
TWEAK: Instead of soaking the bread in milk, fry the little pieces to make croutons.
TOMORROW: Pick out any mozzarella and set aside; gently cook any leftovers until soft and reduced for a lovely pasta sauce.

WARM BUTTERNUT SQUASH SALAD WITH LABNEH AND CHILLI

SERVES 4–6

500g/1lb 2oz/2 cups natural yogurt

salt and pepper

1 small butternut squash or pumpkin

olive oil

a few sprigs of thyme, leaves only

1 red chilli, deseeded and finely chopped

For the dressing

a big bunch of parsley, leaves only

½ tsp ground coriander

1 garlic clove, peeled and crushed to a paste

juice of ½ lemon

100ml/3½fl oz/7 tbsp olive oil

Labneh is yogurt that has been strained of all its whey, leaving the thick, almost cheesy, curd behind. It needs a day or two to reach its peak, so if you're making this at more of a run, just use a really thick, Greek-style yogurt.

1–2 DAYS AHEAD:

Line a bowl with a clean tea towel. Tip the yogurt in, add a pinch of salt, then tie the towel up with string and hang from a cupboard handle over the bowl.

UP TO A DAY AHEAD:

Preheat the oven to 200°C/400°F/Gas mark 6. Wash the squash but don't peel it (the skin is delicious) and cut it into rounds, discarding the seeds. Toss with olive oil, salt, pepper and thyme, and roast for 45 minutes. Leave to cool; chill overnight if necessary.

UP TO AN HOUR AHEAD:

Make the dressing: finely chop the parsley and mix with the ground coriander, garlic, lemon juice, olive oil and salt and pepper, or whiz in a blender.

30 MINUTES AHEAD:

If necessary, warm the squash in a medium oven (180°C/350°F/ Gas mark 4). If the oven's already on for something else, do it at that temperature, keeping an eye on it if it's particularly hot.

DINNERTIME:

Place the chunks of squash on a plate and top with a dollop of labneh. Scatter with chopped chilli and a generous dressing of parsley oil, then serve.

TWEAK: Use goat's milk yogurt instead, to produce lovely goat's curd. Also delicious just spread on toast.

TOMORROW: Perk up leftover labneh with herbs and garlic for a sort of homemade Boursin.

TOMATO
TARTE TATIN

SERVES 6–8

100/3½oz/7 tbsp butter

4 onions, peeled and
    thinly sliced

2 tsp thyme leaves,
    finely chopped

salt and pepper

1 garlic clove, peeled
    and finely sliced

1 tbsp sugar

600g/1lb 5oz cherry tomatoes,
    halved

300g/10½oz puff pastry

To serve

salad leaves

olive oil

The alliteration of this dish isn't entirely accidental, or at least it wasn't when I first ate it. My cake-maker friend Victoria Glass ran a supper club based on letters of the alphabet, and I was lucky enough to be there for the 'T' night. We ate tripe tempura, teal, tartiflette, tail, tongue and testicle terrine, treacle tart, tiramisu and, somewhere in there, a tomato tarte Tatin. Victoria did it with a cute cherry tomato toffee apple, a clear tomato soup, and a tomato and Tabasco granita. This is a simplified version, though if you ask Victoria nicely, I'm sure she'll let you in on the rest. Her website is victorias-alphabet-soup.blogspot.com.

You can make the tart a day ahead, and it's up to you whether you serve it warm or cold.

UP TO A DAY AHEAD:

Melt half the butter in a 25cm/10in diameter tarte Tatin pan or similarly sized ovenproof frying pan, and add the onions and thyme. Season with salt and pepper, and cook over a low heat for a good 30 minutes, stirring occasionally, until caramelized and glossy. Add the garlic and cook for a further minute or two, then tip onto a plate and set aside.

Put the remaining butter in the pan and melt over a medium heat, then add the sugar and stir until dissolved. Gently simmer until lightly browned, then lay in the cherry tomatoes, cut side down. Cook for 5 minutes, keeping an eye on the pan to ensure you don't burn the butter. Take the pan off the heat and spoon the onions over the tomatoes.

Roll out the pastry to a circle a touch larger than your pan, prick all over with a fork, and pop in the fridge for 20 minutes. Preheat the oven to 180°C/350°F/Gas mark 4.

Lay the pastry over the tomatoes and onions and tuck in at the edges. Bake for 20 minutes, until the pastry is puffed and golden. Leave to cool, then carefully invert onto a plate. You may need to redistribute some of the tomatoes: this is not a failing. Cover and chill.

1 HOUR AHEAD:

Take the tart out of the fridge. If you want to serve it warm, preheat the oven to 180°C/350°F/Gas mark 4 and put the tart on a baking sheet, giving it a 5–10 minute blast in the oven.

DINNERTIME:

Serve the tart with a few salad leaves and a drizzle of olive oil.

TART: A few shavings of Parmesan at the end will add a good tang and salty edge.

TWEAK: Use slices of normal tomato instead of cherry tomatoes.

TOMORROW: Store in the fridge. It will keep for a few days.

RABBIT IN A HAT

SERVES 4–6

olive oil
100g/3½oz chorizo, diced
2 rabbit legs, on the bone
1 onion, peeled and
    finely chopped
1 garlic clove, peeled and
    finely sliced
1 stick of celery, trimmed and
    finely chopped
salt and pepper
150ml/5fl oz/⅔ cup dry sherry
300ml/10fl oz/1¼ cups chicken
    stock
25g/1oz/2 tbsp butter
150g/5½oz filo pastry
a bunch of parsley

TART: I added a splash of
cream to this the first time
I made it, which adds richness
should the rest of the meal be
relatively light.

TWEAK: The stew makes
a lovely meal for two with
some new potatoes or rice
and a green salad. Or turn it
upside down and put a puff
pastry lid on top. Instead of
rabbit you could use chicken
thighs and legs.

TOMORROW: Leftovers make
a very good pasta sauce,
and freeze well. You'll also
likely have half a pack of filo
pastry left over: it freezes well.

We served this dish, along with the flowers up a sleeve (p.86), at the Secret Larder when magician Drum Money-Coutts performed for the guests. Though I dare say his ability to guess people's pin codes and make cards appear in their wallets was more impressive than the food, this dish went down extremely well.

The stew will benefit from being made a day ahead. See pp.76–77 for a photograph of the finished dish.

UP TO A DAY AHEAD:

Heat a little oil in a wide saucepan over a medium heat and cook the chorizo until crisp. Using a slotted spoon, transfer to a plate. Increase the temperature and brown the rabbit legs on both sides, then remove to the plate with the chorizo. Now turn the heat down to low and add the onion, garlic and celery. Season with salt and plenty of pepper, cover and gently sweat for 10–15 minutes, until softened. Add the sherry and simmer, uncovered, over a medium heat for a few minutes. Return the chorizo and rabbit to the pan, along with the stock. Bring to a boil, cover and cook over a low heat for 1½ hours.

By now, the rabbit meat should be coming away from the bone, so remove from the pan and set aside for 5 minutes. Pull the meat apart using a pair of forks, and return to the pan. Simmer uncovered for 15 minutes, stirring occasionally, until the liquid has reduced and the meat is well shredded, then leave to cool. Chill overnight.

Preheat the oven to 180°C/350°F/Gas mark 4. Melt the butter in a small saucepan. Lay 3–4 sheets of filo pastry on top of each other and brush lavishly with butter, then cut into 4–6 squares. Push each square into a deep muffin tin and bake for 10 minutes, until golden. Store in an airtight container.

30 MINUTES AHEAD:

Reheat the stew over a medium-low heat, stirring occasionally. Finely chop the parsley. Taste the stew for seasoning and adjust if necessary.

DINNERTIME:

Stir the parsley through the stew. Put a filo 'hat' on each plate and fill with the rabbit. Serve.

FRIED PIG CHEEKS WITH GRIBICHE

SERVES 6

500g/1lb 2oz pig cheeks
½ onion
1 carrot
1 garlic clove, peeled and
    squashed with the flat of
    a knife
1 bay leaf
a few sprigs of thyme
150ml/5fl oz/⅔ cup dry white
    wine
salt and black peppercorns
a bunch of parsley,
    finely chopped
2 eggs
2 tbsp flour, seasoned with
    salt and pepper
50g/1¾oz/½ cup dried
    breadcrumbs
olive oil
salad leaves, to serve

For the gribiche

1 egg
1 tbsp Dijon mustard
100ml/3½fl oz/7 tbsp
    vegetable oil
1 shallot, peeled and
    finely chopped
3 tbsp finely chopped gherkin
2 tbsp finely chopped capers
2 tsp finely chopped tarragon
½ lemon

Another recipe with pig cheeks. I really can't get enough of them, though if you can, use skinless pork belly here instead, and make scratchings (p.28) with the skin.

The prepared cheeks will sit happily overnight in the fridge. Then all you have to do is fry them 10 minutes before serving.

UP TO A DAY AHEAD:

Put the pig cheeks, onion, carrot, garlic, bay, thyme and wine in a saucepan and cover with water. Lob in a few peppercorns and a generous pinch of salt, and bring to a boil. Skim off any scum that rises and gently simmer for 1½ hours, until very tender.

Remove the cheeks from the stock and cool for 15 minutes, then shred them thoroughly in a bowl using a couple of forks. Add the chopped parsley, one of the eggs and a splash of the cooking liquor. Season with salt and pepper to taste and stir to combine. Form into 6 neat patties, cover and chill for at least 30 minutes.

Put the seasoned flour in a bowl. Put the remaining egg in another bowl and beat. Put the breadcrumbs in a third bowl. Coat each patty in flour, then egg, then breadcrumbs. Cover and return to the fridge.

To make the gribiche, boil the egg for 6 minutes, then pop into a bowl of cold water. Once cool, peel and halve. Remove the yolk and mash in a bowl. Mix with the mustard, then slowly pour in the oil, whisking to emulsify. Finely chop the egg white and add, along with the shallot, gherkin, capers, tarragon and a squeeze of lemon juice. Check for seasoning, cover and refrigerate.

1 HOUR AHEAD:

Take the pig cheek patties out of the fridge.

10 MINUTES AHEAD:

Heat a good slug of oil in a frying pan over a medium heat. Fry the pig cheeks for 3 minutes on each side, until crisp and golden.

DINNERTIME:

Serve the pig cheeks with the gribiche and a few salad leaves.

TART: For a punchier salad, toss a few parsley – or perhaps lovage – leaves with finely sliced shallot and lemon juice.
TWEAK: A decent ready-made tartare sauce will work in place of the gribiche if you're short on time.
TOMORROW: Leftover gribiche goes very well alongside a game terrine or some asparagus.

OYSTER PO' BOYS

SERVES 6

a few good shakes of
    Tabasco sauce
6 tbsp mayonnaise
    (homemade or
    shop-bought)
2 sweet pickled gherkins,
    finely chopped
1 Little Gem lettuce
12 oysters
2 eggs, beaten
500ml/18fl oz/generous 2 cups
    vegetable or sunflower oil
1 baguette
100g/3½oz/generous ¾ cup
    polenta (cornmeal)
1 tsp paprika or
    Cajun seasoning
lemon wedges, to serve

Each year my friend Edu Hawkins exhibits at the Secret Larder his extraordinary photographs (see p.140) from the New Orleans Jazz Festival, while I do a menu to match. The food of New Orleans, and the American South in general, is great fun to cook, largely straightforward and, for the most part, cheap, and while oysters aren't seen as the frugal ingredient they once were, they're still fairly thrifty when you're serving just a couple each, as you are here. The traditional Louisiana po'boy is a substantial stuffed baguette: this interpretation is downsized to fit into a dinner menu.

While there are elements of this you can prepare in advance, I should warn you that if you are of a nervous disposition when it comes to shucking oysters, you'd be advised to have a main course and pud that are well within your comfort zone if you're serving this as a starter. But I promise it's worth it.

UP TO 6 HOURS AHEAD:

Stir a few shakes of Tabasco into the mayo, according to taste, and add the chopped gherkins. Cover and refrigerate. Thinly slice and wash the lettuce, then cover and put in the fridge.

30 MINUTES AHEAD:

Shuck the oysters, then coat in the beaten egg. Leave them in the egg for now.

10 MINUTES AHEAD:

Heat the oil in a saucepan or sauté pan over a medium high heat. Slice the baguette. Mix the polenta and paprika in a bowl.

When the oil is hot enough, a piece of bread should sizzle at once and turn golden brown in 30 seconds. One at a time, take an oyster from the egg, shaking off any excess, and roll in the polenta, then put on a plate until they're all done. Fry 6 at a time for 1–2 minutes, until golden and crisp, then, using a slotted spoon, transfer to kitchen paper to drain.

DINNERTIME:

Spread a slice of baguette with the mayonnaise, top with lettuce and a couple of oysters, and serve with lemon wedges.

TART: Lay a couple of slices of tomato on each slice of baguette after spreading with mayonnaise.
TWEAK: If you can't face shucking a dozen oysters with guests about to arrive, use raw prawns or chunks of chicken breast instead and proceed as above, frying for 3–4 minutes.

FARRO RISOTTO WITH BLUE CHEESE AND WALNUTS

SERVES 4–6

olive oil

1 small onion, peeled and
finely chopped

1 stick of celery,
finely chopped

salt and pepper

250g/9oz/1¼ cups farro, spelt
or pearl barley, rinsed
under running water

150ml/5fl oz/⅔ cup dry white
wine

750ml/1¼ pints/3 cups
vegetable or chicken stock

100g/3½oz blue cheese,
such as Stilton, Stichelton
or Gorgonzola

50g/1¾oz/½ cup chopped
walnuts

50g/1¾oz pea shoots

'Is farro the same as spelt?' I wondered as I started writing this recipe. The top entry on Google, an incensed blog post entitled 'FARRO IS NOT SPELT!', rather cleared up the question. They are not, truth told, all that far apart from each other, pearl barley being another near-equivalent, hence the confusion. That said, the texture and nuttiness of farro is particularly suited to a dish like this.

Like the other grains, and unlike rice, it is very difficult to overcook farro. Nor is it necessary to ladle and stir as you would with proper risotto, making it perfect for when you have guests to look after.

UP TO A DAY AHEAD:

Heat a little oil in a saucepan and add the onion and celery. Season with salt and pepper, cover and sweat over a low heat for 10 minutes, until soft. Add the grains and stir to coat, then add the wine and increase the heat. Simmer for a minute or so, stirring, then add the stock. Bring to a boil and simmer over a gentle heat for 45 minutes. Cover and chill, or proceed to dinnertime.

30 MINUTES AHEAD (IF REHEATING):

Put the risotto over a low heat and add a good spoonful of stock or water. Gently reheat, stirring occasionally.

DINNERTIME:

Stir the cheese through the grains and taste for seasoning. Serve the risotto/farrotto garnished with chopped walnuts, a few pea shoots and a drizzle of olive oil.

TART: For a main course, serve with roast chicken or guinea fowl (p.144).

TWEAK: For a meaty version, crumble in some spicy Italian sausage along with the farro.

TOMORROW: This will keep for a couple of days in the fridge, and makes a good desk lunch.

ROAST BONE MARROW WITH CHILLI AND GARLIC BREADCRUMBS

SERVES 4

8 x 8cm/about 3in centre cut
    veal marrow bones,
    halved vertically
50g/1¾oz/1 cup fresh
    breadcrumbs
1 garlic clove, peeled and
    crushed to a paste
1 chilli, deseeded and
    finely chopped
a small bunch of parsley,
    finely chopped
zest of ½ lemon
2 tbsp olive oil
salt and pepper

There are certain things that, if found on a menu, I am unable to resist. Snails with butter and garlic, crisp calamari with aioli, beetroot in pretty much any which way it comes, a negroni cocktail... their magnetism is almost always overwhelming. But next to bone marrow they are as pale and milky as a pail of milk.

It's the rich, gelatinous, gooey, spreadable unctuousness that does it, the sheer decadence of the stuff. And yet it is cheap to buy and easy to prepare, once you've tracked some down. You'll need to call the butcher and ask him or her for centre-cut veal bones, about 8cm/3in long, and halved down the middle. That last bit isn't vital but it makes them easier to serve. Order them for the day you're going to eat them, as they spoil easily.

The topping can be prepared several hours ahead, so when your guests arrive all you have to do is pop the bones in the oven. Serve with plenty of toasted sourdough bread.

UP TO 3 HOURS AHEAD:
Combine the breadcrumbs, garlic, chilli, parsley, lemon zest and olive oil, and season with salt and pepper.

40 MINUTES AHEAD:
Preheat the oven to 200°C/400°F/Gas mark 6. A cooler oven is fine if you're cooking other things in there, though the marrow will need longer. Put the bones, marrow side up, in a roasting pan and top with the breadcrumbs. Roast for 15–20 minutes, until golden.

DINNERTIME:
Serve with toast.

TART: At his London restaurant, St John, Fergus Henderson serves bone marrow with a parsley and shallot salad. I'd ditch the chilli if you choose to do this.

TWEAK: If you can't get the bones halved, follow the above recipe, standing the bones upright in the oven instead.

TOMORROW: The bones spoil very easily, so either use for stock immediately or freeze.

ORANGE, FENNEL AND JUNIPER-CURED SALMON WITH PICKLED BEETROOT AND HORSERADISH

SERVES 6–10

600g/1lb 5oz salmon
50g/1¾oz rock salt
50g/1¾oz smoked salt (or alternatively just use 100g/3½oz rock salt)
150g/5½oz/¾ cup molasses sugar or soft dark brown sugar
1 tsp peppercorns, crushed
2 tsp fennel seeds, crushed
1 tbsp juniper berries
zest of 1 orange
a small bunch of dill

For the pickled beetroot

500g/1lb 2oz cooked beetroot, finely sliced or cubed
200ml/7fl oz/generous ¾ cup white wine vinegar
200g/7oz/1 cup caster (superfine) sugar
1 shallot, peeled and finely sliced

To serve

salad leaves, ideally pea shoots or watercress
microherbs such as amaranth or cress (optional)
fresh horseradish root or horseradish sauce
olive oil
lemon or orange wedges

Cured fish is a very nifty dish to have up your do-ahead sleeve. Whether it's this salt-and-spice-cured salmon, or the soused herring on p.84, it's something very simple that you can do several days in advance and then forget about, at least for the time being.

You may prefer a lighter cure, in which case 24 hours is ample, but this can be done up to 72 hours ahead. The pickled beetroot (a very handy thing to have on standby) will keep for months.

Serve with toasted rye bread (p.19) and butter.

1–3 DAYS AHEAD:

To cure the salmon, blend all the salt, sugar, spices, orange zest and dill in a food processor, or alternatively crush the spices and chop the dill before combining in a bowl. Scatter a layer of the cure in a non-metallic dish (metal may react), then lay the fish on top, skin side down. Blanket thoroughly with the rest of the cure, then cover with clingfilm and place something heavy on top – a plate and a can of beans, for example. Refrigerate.

To make the pickled beetroot, put the vinegar and sugar in a saucepan over a low heat, until the sugar has dissolved. Bring to a boil, add the shallot and simmer for 5 minutes, then pour over the sliced beetroot. Store in sterilized jars (see note on p.2).

UP TO 3 HOURS AHEAD:

Remove the salmon from the fridge and scrape away the salt crust. Using a very sharp knife, cut thin slices of salmon away from the skin and lay on a plate. Cover and chill.

30 MINUTES AHEAD:

Remove the salmon from the fridge.

DINNERTIME:

Arrange slices of cured salmon on a plate and garnish with leaves, pickled beetroot and either freshly grated horseradish or a dollop of horseradish sauce. Finish with a flick of olive oil and a lemon or orange wedge, and serve.

TWEAK: The cure is almost infinitely tweakable. Keep roughly the same proportions of sugar to salt and then play around with the rest – grated beetroot will add a lovely pink blush to the flesh, while a big bunch of dill produces a more traditional gravadlax.

TOMORROW: Pickled beetroot is delicious with any goat's cheese, or alongside a pork pie. Leftover salmon can be tossed through salads, eaten on toast, or indeed frozen.

SOUSED HERRING WITH WARM POTATO AND DILL VODKA

SERVES 6

3 tbsp olive oil

100ml/3½fl oz/7 tbsp white wine vinegar

zest and juice of 1 lemon

2 shallots, peeled and finely sliced

1 tsp juniper berries, lightly crushed

a small bunch of dill, roughly chopped

6 herring fillets

For the dill vodka

300ml/10fl oz/1¼ cups vodka

50g/1¾oz/¼ cup caster (superfine) sugar

a bunch of dill

For the dressing

1 tsp sour cream

2 tsp grainy mustard

1 tbsp white wine vinegar

2 tbsp olive oil

salt and pepper

To serve

3 large new potatoes

salad leaves

If you haven't tried sousing your own fish before, then this is a good place to start. It's the easiest thing to do and people tend to be impressed that you've bothered in the first place. The beauty of this is that you can do it days in advance, though for a lighter cure I favour 24–48 hours.

This recipe was inspired by Andrew Pern at the Star Inn in Harome, North Yorkshire.

1–7 DAYS AHEAD:

Put the oil, vinegar, lemon zest and juice, shallots, juniper and dill in a saucepan and bring to a boil. Simmer for 5 minutes then leave to cool completely. Put the herring in a non-metallic dish or jar and pour over the sousing liquor. Cover and refrigerate.

To make the dill vodka, mix the vodka, sugar and dill in a small saucepan and gently warm until about bathwater temperature, stirring to dissolve the sugar. Cool, bottle and refrigerate.

UP TO 6 HOURS AHEAD:

Make the dressing: mix the sour cream, mustard, vinegar and olive oil. Season with salt and pepper and set aside.

UP TO 1 HOUR AHEAD:

Bring the potatoes to a boil in a pan of salted water. Simmer for 15–20 minutes, until easily pierced with a knife. Drain and leave in the pan, covered with a lid to keep the warmth in. Put 6 shot glasses in the freezer.

DINNERTIME:

Slice the cooked potatoes in half lengthways and put on 6 plates. Top with a fillet of soused herring and a few of the soused shallots and garnish with salad leaves. Finish with a spoonful of dressing and serve with a shot of chilled dill vodka.

TART: Cube the cooked potato and mix with diced apple, crème fraîche, grainy mustard and chopped dill – *à la* Andrew Pern.

TWEAK: Herring aren't always easy to find, so you could use mackerel instead, or indeed any firm-fleshed white fish.

TOMORROW: The herring will keep for several weeks, should you fancy making a bigger batch.

SMOKED SALMON TARTARE WITH PICKLED CUCUMBER

SERVES 6

500g/1lb 2oz smoked salmon
150g/5½oz crème fraîche
juice of 1 lemon
a small handful of chives,
    finely chopped
black pepper
For the cucumber pickle
250g/9oz/1¼ cups caster
    (superfine) sugar
200ml/7fl oz/generous ¾ cup
    white wine vinegar or
    cider vinegar
1 cucumber
2 shallots, peeled and
    finely sliced
a small bunch of dill, chopped

We made the arguably brave/foolhardy decision to host a hen party as a private event at the supper club a couple of years ago. This involved, as you might expect, suggestively shaped straws, a modestly dressed waiter named Tony, and a lot of serious and contrived concentration on the cooking while goodness-knows-what was going on behind me. This was the starter and it was such a success with the girls that they asked for the recipe for the wedding party.

The salmon tartare is a do-ahead doddle, and while the pickled cucumber loses its colour after a few hours, this doesn't matter if you're dining by candlelight.

Serve with hot toast and salty butter.

UP TO A DAY AHEAD:

Skin the smoked salmon if necessary, then chop into small pieces. Mix with the crème fraîche, lemon juice and chives, and season with plenty of black pepper. Cover and chill.

1 HOUR AHEAD:

You can make the cucumber pickle further ahead if you like, though the cucumber quickly loses colour. Up to you. Stir the sugar and vinegar together until the sugar has dissolved. Finely slice the cucumber and combine with the shallots and dill in a bowl, then pour over the vinegar mixture.

DINNERTIME:

Toast some bread and serve the smoked salmon tartare with the pickled cucumber and toast.

TART: Smoked fish and horseradish always get on terrifically well, so try bunging in some freshly grated horseradish or a dollop of horseradish sauce with the salmon tartare.

TWEAK: Instead of the pickled cucumber, serve this with pickled beetroot (p.83).

TOMORROW: Leftover salmon is delicious tossed through pasta with a slug of olive oil. Pickled cucumber will keep almost indefinitely, although it will lose its emerald gleam.

STUFFED COURGETTE BLOSSOMS
(FLOWERS UP A SLEEVE)

SERVES 6

a good handful of fresh
  breadcrumbs
a handful of black olives
6 courgette (zucchini)
  blossoms, still attached to
  small courgettes if possible
3 medium courgettes
  (zucchini)
juice of 1 lemon
salt and pepper
edible flowers or microherbs
  (optional)
For the stuffing
2 tbsp olive oil
1 onion, peeled and
  finely chopped
1 garlic clove, peeled and
  crushed to a paste
1 tsp thyme leaves,
  finely chopped
300g/10½oz soft goat's
  cheese
a handful of parsley,
  finely chopped
zest of 1 lemon
For the dressing
1 tsp Dijon mustard
2 tsp white wine vinegar
4 tsp olive oil

TWEAK: If you can't find
courgette flowers, serve this as
a sort of tagliatelle, tossing the
courgette ribbons with goat's
cheese, olives, breadcrumbs
and the dressing.

TOMORROW: Leftover
stuffing and courgettes will
make a delicious summer
tart. Top rolled puff pastry with
them and bake until golden.

We served this dish to supper club guests when magician Drum
Money-Coutts came to the Secret Larder. It does slightly hinge
on you being able to find courgette flowers, which are around for
much of the summer but which don't tend to be available in your
local supermarket. I order them from Andreas in west London,
which is useful information if you live in the capital, and hopeless
otherwise. All I can advise is that you ring around a few grocers or
butter up a friend with a vegetable patch.

The stuffing, the dressing and the garnish can all be prepared
a day ahead. Then on the day, you'll just need to find 20 minutes
or so to get the courgettes in order.

UP TO A DAY AHEAD:

To make the stuffing, heat the olive oil in a frying pan and gently
cook the onion with the garlic and thyme until softened. Season
with salt and pepper and leave to cool.

Beat the onion mixture into the cheese along with the parsley
and lemon zest, and beat for a minute or two until light and fluffy.
Taste for seasoning, then cover and chill.

To make the dressing, mix the mustard, vinegar and oil.
Season with salt and pepper to taste and store in a jar in the fridge.

Toast the breadcrumbs in a dry frying pan over a medium
heat until golden. Add a pinch of salt and set aside.

Pit the olives by squashing them with the flat of a knife and
removing the stones. Roughly chop and set aside.

UP TO 2 HOURS AHEAD:

Wash the courgette blossoms and check for any critters, then
pat dry. Carefully stuff each flower with a spoonful of the goat's
cheese mixture. Cover and chill.

With a potato peeler, shave the courgettes into ribbons, then
toss with lemon juice and pepper. Cover and set aside.

15 MINUTES AHEAD:

Taking care not to spill the stuffing, wrap a few courgette ribbons
around the courgettes with the stuffed flowers, so as to mimic a
sleeve, and pop on serving plates.

DINNERTIME:

Scatter over toasted breadcrumbs, olives and a few herbs or
flowers, if you like. Finish with the dressing and serve.

MARINATED BAKED GOAT'S CHEESE

SERVES 6

1 small garlic clove, peeled
    and crushed to a paste
1 red chilli, deseeded and
    finely chopped
a few mint leaves, chopped
juice of 1 lemon
100ml/3½fl oz/7 tbsp olive oil
salt and pepper
6 small goat's cheese rounds,
    about 100g/3½oz each
2 large aubergines
    (eggplants)
salad leaves

For some reason, I rarely think to tinker with cheese. It seems to be a tweaker, as opposed to a tweakee – that's to say, you add it to a dish to give that dish a different dimension, rather than adding something to cheese to change its own characteristics. But it's willing to take on other flavours and doing so provides a bit more oomph to a simple starter.

The marinated cheese is wrapped in griddled aubergines, and both elements can be prepared ahead. After that, it's a simple thing to wrap and bake the cheeses. Serve with crusty bread.

UP TO A WEEK AHEAD:

Mix the garlic, chilli, mint, lemon juice and olive oil and season with pepper. Spoon over the cheeses, cover and chill. If short of time, you can push straight on with the rest of the dish.

UP TO A DAY AHEAD:

Thinly slice the aubergines lengthways and fry in batches on a griddle or frying pan until soft and charred. Cool.

30 MINUTES AHEAD:

Preheat the oven to 180°C/350°F/Gas mark 4. Wrap each cheese in a couple of slices of aubergine and place in a baking dish. Bake for 15 minutes and serve with crusty bread and a few salad leaves.

TART: You could give this more of a tricolore angle by layering sliced tomato and basil on either side of the cheese before wrapping in the aubergine.

TWEAK: I've marinated feta in a similar fashion to this, omitting the baking part and instead crumbling the feta over roasted red peppers. Try this with the red pepper stew with 'nduja (p.174).

TOMORROW: Leftover griddled aubergine is a useful thing for any desk lunch, or add it to a vegetarian lasagne.

QUAIL ESCABECHE

SERVES 6

6 quails
salt and pepper
150ml/5fl oz/⅔ cup olive oil
6 onions, peeled and
    finely sliced
100ml/3½fl oz/7 tbsp red
    wine vinegar
zest of 1 orange
100g/3½oz stoned dates,
    finely chopped
100g/3½oz sultanas,
    finely chopped
a big handful of parsley,
    finely chopped
50g/1¾oz skinned hazelnuts,
    roughly chopped
    (optional)

TART: Considering this dish
is believed to be Arabic in
origin, you could definitely
get away with adding some
gentle spices when cooking
the onions – a few strands of
saffron, some roasted ground
cumin, a pinch of ground
cinnamon – and throwing on
a few pomegranate seeds at
the end for good measure.

TWEAK: Try a twist on the
Venetian *sarde in saor* by
replacing the quail with
sardine fillets, tossed in flour
and fried in oil before being
marinated.

TOMORROW: Leftover
escabeche is just the thing
for a picnic.

The relationship between *escabeche* and *ceviche* is an opaque
but interesting one. Certainly there's no denying the etymological
similarities between the two words, particularly when you consider
the eighteenth-century English word used for this preparation –
caveach. Add to this the fact that, gastronomically, both began
as a combination of fish and something acidic – citrus juice or
vinegar – and it's difficult not to bracket them together. There is,
however, a crucial difference, which is that here you're adding
the marinade to cooked meat, as opposed to raw, as well as
adding sweetening undertones.

The quail benefits from its time in the marinade, so this is a
splendid do-ahead starter. Serve with crusty bread and butter.

UP TO 2 DAYS AHEAD:
Preheat the oven to 220°C/425°F/Gas mark 7.

Using a sharp knife or kitchen scissors, cut the quails in half
along the spine and breast bone. Season all over with salt and
pepper, rub with a little of the oil and roast for 15 minutes, skin side
up. Remove and rest.

Meanwhile, make the escabeche. Heat a little of the oil in a
large saucepan over a low heat and add the onions. Season with
salt and pepper and cook for about 45 minutes to 1 hour, stirring
regularly, until they're rich and caramelized.

Stir the vinegar, remaining olive oil, orange zest, dates,
sultanas and parsley through the onions and simmer for
10 minutes, then spoon over the quail. Leave to cool, then cover
and refrigerate.

Toast the hazelnuts, if using, in a dry frying pan over a medium
heat, taking care not to burn them.

1 HOUR AHEAD:
Take the quail out of the fridge.

DINNERTIME:
Serve the escabeche, scattered with toasted hazelnuts if you like.

CEVICHE WITH TORTILLAS

SERVES 6

500g/1lb 2oz sea bass or
    another firm white fish
juice of 4 limes
1 long red chilli, deseeded
    and finely chopped
1 red onion, peeled and very
    finely chopped
1 tsp salt
6 tortillas, or a bag of
    tortilla chips
olive oil
a handful of fresh coriander
    (cilantro)

The idea behind ceviche is that the fish 'cooks' in the citrus juice, giving you something that is zippy and fresh. Of course, that's assuming you begin with fresh fish, which you must. Then it's a doddle in do-ahead cookery. Prep the marinade, slice the fish, introduce the two 30 minutes before serving and bake (or even buy) a few tortillas. What could be easier?

UP TO 6 HOURS AHEAD:
Skin the fish, if necessary, then cut into 1cm/½in dice. Cover and refrigerate.

Mix the lime juice, chilli, onion and salt. Cover and set aside.

Preheat the oven to 180°C/350°F/Gas mark 4. Cut the tortillas into triangles, place on a baking sheet and brush with oil. Bake for 5 minutes until crisp (you may need to do this in batches), sprinkle with salt and set aside.

30 MINUTES AHEAD:
Combine the fish with the marinade, cover and chill.

DINNERTIME:
Put the ceviche in a serving bowl, draining any excess liquid, and scatter over a few coriander leaves. Serve with the tortillas.

TART: There are plenty of ingredients that would respond well to being added to a ceviche, such as chopped tomato or avocado. Try adding some chopped ripe mango for extra sweetness.
TWEAK: When he came to cook at the Secret Larder, Tom Parker Bowles did a delicious St Clement's ceviche, using lemon and orange juice instead of lime.
TOMORROW: The acidity of the lime juice will keep the fish edible for some time, but this is best eaten fresh.

POTTED PORK WITH PICKLED RHUBARB

SERVES 6–8

2 tbsp olive oil

1 onion, peeled and
    finely sliced

1 garlic clove, peeled and
    squashed with the flat
    of a knife

1 stick of celery,
    roughly chopped

salt and pepper

½ carrot

500ml/18fl oz/generous 2 cups
    dry cider

1 smoked ham hock

400g/14oz pork belly,
    skin removed

200g/7oz streaky bacon or
    pancetta, cut into chunks

a sprig of thyme

a bay leaf

a bunch of parsley,
    finely chopped

For the pickled rhubarb

250ml/9fl oz/generous 1 cup
    cider vinegar

300g/10½oz/1½ cups caster
    (superfine) sugar

400g/14oz rhubarb, trimmed
    and finely sliced

a thumb of fresh ginger,
    peeled and chopped
    into matchsticks

1 shallot, peeled and
    finely sliced

This looks lovely served in individual pots, though you could just as well whack the pork into one big pot to take with you on a picnic.

Both the potted pork and pickled rhubarb can be made a week in advance. Serve with toast or crusty baguette.

UP TO A WEEK AHEAD:

Heat the oil in a large saucepan over a medium heat and add the onion, garlic and celery. Season with salt and pepper, and stir for a few minutes until starting to soften, then add the carrot, cider, all the meat, thyme and bay leaf. Top up with water and bring to a boil. Skim off any scum that rises to the top, cover and simmer gently for 3 hours, or transfer to an oven at 160°C/325°F/Gas mark 3.

Remove the meat from the broth and rest for 15 minutes. Pull the hock meat off the bone, discarding the bone and the skin, then shred all the meat together, using a couple of forks. Add the chopped parsley and a couple of spoonfuls of the cooking liquor to bring it all together. Taste for seasoning and add pepper if necessary – it's unlikely to need salt – then press into individual pots or one big pot. Cover and refrigerate.

To make the pickled rhubarb, put the vinegar and sugar in a saucepan over a medium heat and stir until the sugar has dissolved. Bring to a boil, simmer for 3 minutes, then pour over the rhubarb, ginger and shallot. Leave to cool and store in a sterilized jar (see note on p.2).

1 HOUR AHEAD:

Take the potted pork out of the fridge in order for it to come up to room temperature – you don't want it to be fridge-cold.

DINNERTIME:

Serve the pork and the pickled rhubarb with a load of toast and butter.

TART: Mix chopped pistachios through the meat before potting.

TWEAK: You could instead do a sort of potted game number, replacing the ham hock with four duck legs, and the pork belly with diced venison. You'll need to keep the bacon for its fatty binding abilities.

TOMORROW: You will have more pickled rhubarb than you need, but it will keep for months and may be just what you need to lift a sandwich one lunchtime.

CREOLE CHICKEN WITH MARDI GRAS SALAD

SERVES 6

1 tbsp paprika

2 tsp hot cayenne pepper

1 tsp dried oregano

½ tsp salt

1 garlic clove, peeled and crushed to a paste

3 tbsp olive oil

6 chicken thighs

salt and pepper

For the salad

2 corn cobs, or 1 large can (about 350g/12oz) sweetcorn

1 small red onion, peeled and finely sliced

juice of 1 lemon

2 heads of Little Gem lettuce

a handful of fresh coriander (cilantro)

For the dressing

1 egg yolk

2 tsp Dijon mustard

1 tbsp white wine vinegar

4 tbsp olive oil

a few shakes of Tabasco sauce

TART: Add a mix of sliced peppers and green beans to the salad.

TWEAK: Try this with whole poussin instead, bulking up the salad and serving as a main course.

TOMORROW: Leftovers will keep until tomorrow for a desk lunch.

I did this at one of our New Orleans themed evenings, and worried that the Mardi Gras colour scheme of purple, green and gold in the salad was a little bit contrived, but as it happened it worked rather well. The trick is in giving the thinly sliced red onion a decent stint in the lemon juice, to take the edge off. If you've got enough to be getting on with nearer dinner, then you can skip the reheating of the chicken.

UP TO 2 DAYS AHEAD:

Mix the paprika, cayenne, oregano, salt, garlic and olive oil and spread all over the chicken. Cover and chill.

UP TO 6 HOURS AHEAD:

Preheat the oven to 180°C/350°F/Gas mark 4. Put a heavy griddle pan over a high heat and fry the chicken thighs for a couple of minutes on each side, until charred and smoky. Roast in the oven for 45 minutes. Leave to cool for 10 minutes, then shred the meat, discarding skin and bone. Cover and chill.

If using whole corn cobs, remove the husks and stand the cobs upright on a chopping board. Using a sharp knife, slice down the sides to cut the kernels away. Bring a pan of salted water to a boil and simmer the corn for a couple of minutes, then drain and rinse under cold water for 30 seconds. Alternatively, drain a can of sweetcorn.

Mix the onion with the lemon juice, cover and set aside.

To make the dressing, whisk together the egg yolk, mustard and vinegar, and then slowly whisk in the olive oil and finally add the Tabasco. Taste for seasoning, cover and chill.

30 MINUTES AHEAD:

Take the chicken and the dressing out of the fridge. Separate and wash the lettuce leaves.

10 MINUTES AHEAD (OPTIONAL):

Heat a drop of oil in a frying pan over a medium-high heat and fry the chicken until crisped and golden.

Roughly chop the coriander. Toss together the red onion, sweetcorn, lettuce, most of the coriander and the dressing.

DINNERTIME:

Arrange the salad on plates and top with the chicken. Garnish with the remaining coriander and serve.

Mains

When it comes to main courses, I always think the Italians have it right – a good piece of meat or fish, cooked without too much fuss, served with some seasonal, cared-for vegetables. I suppose that's traditionally the British way, too, though often there seems to be the impression that 1) it isn't a proper meal without potatoes, and 2) meat and two veg is far too conservative, the meat needing at least four satellites for it to be considered a complete dish. Nonsense of course – a generous central monolith only needs one or two additional elements to act as supports. The braised shin of beef (p.137), for example, does not need peas and carrots and potatoes and pastry to complete it, rather just a few spring greens (p.167), a good mash or a hunk of bread and a pot of mustard.

Indeed, serving any meat at all isn't a necessity. There seem to be more vegetarians about these days, and even if they don't happen to be sitting at your table, it's good for the health and the wallet to swerve the meat aisle every once in a while. The vegetarian mains here are, I hope, punchy enough for you not to find yourself yearning for a lump of cow.

One difficulty with mains is that, unless slow-cooked or served cold, there is almost always a bit of last-minute cooking to do. You can't really, for example, cook a piece of bream in advance and reheat it. So if you are doing something that warrants last-minute cooking, make sure you've got all your ducks in a row before the masses arrive. Then it's just a case of popping it in the oven or into a pan and forgetting about it just long enough to look after your guests, but not for so long that you cremate it. It's not a particularly fine line, and you'll find that most dishes are more forgiving than you think.

ROAST ACORN SQUASH WITH WHITE RISOTTO AND HERB BREADCRUMBS

SERVES 6

olive oil

2 shallots, peeled and
finely chopped

1 stick of celery,
finely chopped

1 garlic clove, peeled and
finely chopped

salt and pepper

1.5 litres/2½ pints/generous
6 cups vegetable or
chicken stock

400g/14oz risotto rice

150ml/5fl oz/⅔ cup dry white
wine or vermouth

50g/1¾oz/4 tbsp butter

50g/1¾oz Parmesan cheese,
grated

For the squash

6 acorn, harlequin, or other
small squash

2 tsp finely chopped thyme
leaves

For the herb breadcrumbs

50g/1¾oz/½ cup dried
breadcrumbs

15g/½oz parsley leaves,
finely chopped

2 sage leaves, finely chopped

1 tsp finely chopped rosemary

The traditional cooking method for risotto makes it pretty much anathema to any concept of do-ahead cookery. There is too much time spent standing over the stove stirring and sweating to be able to look after guests, let alone organise the other elements of the meal. Happily, no great harm is done by cooking it three-quarters of the way in advance, then adding a slosh of stock, butter and Parmesan a few minutes before serving.

Served in 'bowls' of baked squash, it doesn't need much in the way of accompaniment, though perhaps something fresh and green afterwards might be an idea – try the spring greens on p.167, substituting the anchovy for chopped red chilli.

UP TO A DAY AHEAD:

Heat a slug of oil in a large saucepan over a low heat, and add the shallots, celery and garlic. Season well with salt and pepper, cover and sweat for 10 minutes, until softened. Keep an eye on the heat and stir occasionally: you don't want them to change colour. Meanwhile, heat the stock to just below a simmer.

Whack up the heat under the pan of shallots and add the rice. Stir for about a minute before adding the wine or vermouth and then, a minute or so later, a ladle of the hot stock. Continue to stir, adding a ladle of stock any time the rice looks dry, for about 15 minutes and/or until you've used about three-quarters of the stock. Remove from the heat and tip onto a baking sheet – this helps it cool faster, and prevents overcooking. Once cool, cover and refrigerate until needed.

UP TO 6 HOURS AHEAD:

Cut the tops off the squash and scoop out the seeds. Trim their bottoms so they sit flat, if necessary, then put the squash 'bowls' on a baking sheet ready for the oven.

1½ HOURS AHEAD:

Take the risotto out of the fridge. Preheat the oven to 200°C/400°F/ Gas mark 6. Scatter the thyme leaves over the squash and season with salt and pepper, then finish with a flick of oil.

45 MINUTES AHEAD:

Stick the squash in the oven and bake until tender.

Toast the breadcrumbs and herbs in a dry frying pan over a medium heat until golden – a pinch of salt will liven it up. Set aside.

15 MINUTES AHEAD:

Heat the remaining stock to simmering point. Tip the risotto into a saucepan and add the stock. Stir over a medium heat for 5 minutes, until fully cooked. Beat in the butter and Parmesan.

DINNERTIME:

Serve the risotto in the roasted squash bowls with a generous sprinkling of the toasted herb breadcrumbs and a twist of pepper.

TART: Risotto makes a willing canvas for all manner of tarting. I'm very fond of adding cooked and grated beetroot, and swapping the Parmesan for goat's cheese and a dollop of crème fraîche. Or indeed just adding goat's cheese along with the Parmesan.

TWEAK: Instead of the herb breadcrumbs, garnish the dish with a few fried sage leaves.

TOMORROW: With leftover risotto try arancini eggs (p.38). You can even use any leftover breadcrumbs for the crust.

BAKED AUBERGINE WITH GIANT COUSCOUS, LABNEH AND POMEGRANATE

SERVES 6

500g/1lb 2oz/2 cups Greek-
style yogurt
salt and pepper
3 large or 6 smallish
aubergines (eggplants)
1 tsp ground cumin
2 tsp ground coriander
1 tsp sweet smoked paprika
1 garlic clove, peeled and
crushed to a paste
1 red chilli, deseeded and
finely chopped
a big bunch of parsley,
finely chopped
zest and juice of 1 lemon
100ml/3½fl oz/7 tbsp olive oil
1 pomegranate

For the couscous

olive oil
300g/10½oz/1¾ cups giant
couscous
500ml/18fl oz/generous 2 cups
water or vegetable stock
zest and juice of ½ lemon
2 spring onions (scallions),
finely sliced
a handful of fresh coriander
(cilantro), to serve

TWEAK: Use normal couscous
if you can't find the giant stuff,
or instead try bulgur wheat.
TOMORROW: You're likely to
have pomegranate seeds left
over, which you can add to
your breakfast or whiz up to
make juice. Labneh is good
slathered on toast with olive
oil and a rub of garlic.

There's a good reason for the aubergine's affinity with vegetarian dishes. It is both pleasingly substantial and substantially meaty, even responding well to the same treatment as a steak – that's to say, being slapped onto a hot grill until charred and smoky. Its absorbent flesh makes it a willing receiver of punchy marinades and dressings. All in all, a fine specimen.

Labneh is a DIY soft cheese that needs to be made a day or two ahead. You can slather the aubergines with the spice paste and get them oven-ready, and also get the tricky business of extracting the pomegranate seeds out of the way. On the day, it's just aubergines in the oven, couscous in the pan, and you're done.

1–2 DAYS AHEAD:
Line a bowl with a clean tea towel or muslin. Tip in the yogurt along with a good pinch of salt, give it a stir, then tie up the tea towel with string and hang from a cupboard handle over the bowl.

UP TO A DAY AHEAD:
Cut the aubergines in half lengthways and slash the flesh a few times. Mix the spices with the garlic, chilli, parsley, lemon zest and juice, and stir in the olive oil. Season with salt and pepper and spread all over the cut side of the aubergines. Place in an oven-proof dish, cover with foil and chill.

Deseed the pomegranate by halving it and popping out the seeds into a bowl of water – the pith will float and the seeds will sink. Discard the pith, drain the seeds, cover and chill.

1 HOUR AHEAD:
Preheat the oven to 200°C/400°F/Gas mark 6. Bake aubergines for 35 minutes, remove foil and bake for a further 10 minutes, until tender when prodded with a sharp knife. Pick the coriander leaves.

15 MINUTES AHEAD:
Warm the stock to just below a simmer. Heat a little oil in a frying pan over a medium heat, add the couscous and cook for a couple of minutes, stirring regularly. Add the stock and continue to stir until absorbed. Check the couscous and if it's still a little hard, then add more water and continue to cook until soft. Add the lemon zest and juice and the spring onions. Season to taste.

DINNERTIME:
Serve the aubergines on the couscous with a dollop of labneh, a handful of pom seeds and a scattering of coriander leaves.

POTATO RÖSTI WITH A POACHED DUCK EGG AND WILD MUSHROOMS

SERVES 6

3 large, floury potatoes, such as Maris Piper or King Edward
olive oil
2 onions, peeled and finely sliced
salt and pepper
15g/½oz chives, finely sliced
6 duck eggs
25g/1oz/2 tbsp butter
150g/5½oz chanterelles or other wild mushrooms, roughly chopped if large
1 garlic clove, peeled and finely chopped
a handful of parsley, finely chopped
a squeeze of lemon juice
50g/1¾oz watercress

TART: For a non-veggie version, slices of black pudding, fried until crisp and sticky, would work extremely well here.

TWEAK: You can use normal hens' eggs, though they'll need only 3 minutes' poaching. Try making the rösti with sweet potato, or a mixture of root vegetables.

TOMORROW: Leftover mushrooms lend themselves very well to pasta or risotto.

A couple of years ago, my wife Rosie and I spent a gruelling but enjoyable weekend cooking in a tent at the riotously fun Abergavenny Food Festival. I had forgotten that there were two vegetarians one night, and hurried to a farm shop to see what I could dig out. A box of fresh duck eggs and a punnet of chanterelles were my fortuitous finds, and this the resulting dish.

The rösti – fried potato cakes – can be cooked several hours in advance and reheated, as can the poached eggs; I also inspect the mushrooms to check that they're free of grit and bugs, and chop the garlic and parsley, to minimize last-minute fuss.

UP TO 6 HOURS AHEAD:

Boil the potatoes in salted water until cooked, about 30 minutes. Meanwhile, heat a little oil in a frying pan over a medium-low heat and add the onions. Season and cook, stirring occasionally, for 15–20 minutes, until softened and lightly caramelized.

When the potatoes are cooked, drain and cool for a few minutes, then grate into a bowl. Add the chives and the cooked onions and stir through. Taste for seasoning, add salt and pepper if necessary, then form into 6 patties. Cover and chill for 30 minutes.

Heat a good splosh of oil in a non-stick frying pan and fry the patties for a couple of minutes on each side, until crisp and golden. (You may need to do this in batches.) Cover and set aside.

Fill a bowl with cold water and a few ice cubes. Bring a pan of water to a boil and poach the duck eggs in batches of two, for 4 minutes. Using a slotted spoon, plunge them into the iced water. When completely cold, carefully transfer to a tray, cover and chill.

30 MINUTES AHEAD:

Preheat the oven to 180°C/350°F/Gas mark 4.

15 MINUTES AHEAD:

Put the rösti in the oven. Bring a pan of water to a boil. Melt the butter in a sauté pan over a medium heat and add the mushrooms. Season with salt and pepper and cook for 5 minutes or so, until soft and golden. Toss in the garlic, parsley and lemon juice, and cook for another minute, shuggling the pan regularly.

DINNERTIME:

Plunge the poached eggs into boiling water for 30 seconds, then drain on kitchen paper and serve on the rösti, with a spoonful of mushrooms and a peppery and prettifying tangle of watercress.

SHALLOT TARTS WITH TALEGGIO AND PINE NUTS

SERVES 6

50g/1¾oz/4 tbsp butter
6 banana or echalion shallots (the long ones), halved through the root and peeled
salt and pepper
2 tsp finely chopped fresh thyme
100ml/3½fl oz/7 tbsp sherry vinegar
50g/1¾oz/¼ cup caster (superfine) sugar
375g/13oz puff pastry
200g/7oz Taleggio cheese
1 egg, lightly beaten
a handful of pine nuts

Taleggio cheese has a punchy aroma that belies a relatively mild and surprisingly sweet flavour. It melts like a dream and goes well alongside the acidic tang of shallot and buttery puff pastry. These little tarts are an ideal do-ahead lunch or dinner: you can cook the shallots and lay them on the rolled-out pastry, ready to pop into the oven at an hour's notice.

UP TO A DAY AHEAD:

Melt the butter in a wide frying pan or sauté pan over a medium-low heat and add the shallots, cut side down. Season with salt and pepper and cook for 10 minutes, until golden. Turn them over and add the thyme, vinegar and sugar. Give the pan a shake to dissolve the sugar, cover and cook for another 10 minutes, until the shallots are cooked through. Leave to cool.

Divide the pastry into 6 pieces and roll out to rough circle or square shapes. Top with the cold shallots, then break over pieces of the cheese and crimp the sides of the pastry to form a rim. Cover and chill.

1 HOUR AHEAD:

Preheat the oven to 180°C/350°F/Gas mark 4. Brush the edges of the pastry with a little beaten egg, then bake for 25 minutes. Meanwhile, toast the pine nuts in a dry frying pan for a couple of minutes, taking care not to burn them, then set aside.

DINNERTIME:

Scatter a few pine nuts over each tart and serve the tarts with a salad of bitter leaves such as chicory and rocket.

TART: Add a few slices of griddled asparagus and half a boiled and peeled quail egg to each tart before serving.
TWEAK: Instead of individual tarts, make one large one and serve in slices. You could try it with different cheeses – a blue cheese or a goat's cheese, for example.

SPICED VEGETABLES WITH A BAKED EGG

SERVES 6

olive oil

2 red onions, peeled
   and sliced

salt and pepper

2 garlic cloves, peeled and
   crushed to a paste

1 red chilli, deseeded and
   finely chopped

2 tsp ground coriander

1 tsp ground cumin

½ tsp ground allspice

¼ tsp ground cloves

2 x 400g/14oz cans chopped
   tomatoes

1 tsp dried oregano

1 tbsp red wine vinegar

1 tbsp sugar

3 red peppers, deseeded
   and quartered

2 aubergines (eggplants),
   sliced

3 courgettes (zucchini), sliced

6 eggs

To serve

chopped parsley

plain yogurt

flatbreads (shop-bought
   or p.18)

From a purely aesthetic point of view, this is most successful if you have individual dishes; however, it's perfectly doable with a large baking dish and a bit of care when serving – ideally everyone should have an intact egg on their plate at the beginning of dinner.

The spiced vegetables will only improve by being made a day in advance, allowing all the flavours to become acquainted.

UP TO 2 DAYS AHEAD:

Heat a slug of oil in a large saucepan over a medium-low heat and add the onions. Season with salt and pepper, and cook gently for 10–12 minutes, until softened. Add the garlic, chilli and spices, and stir over a medium heat for a minute or so, then chuck in the tomatoes, oregano, vinegar and sugar. Leave to simmer gently.

Meanwhile, put a griddle pan over a high heat with a little oil, and grill the red peppers, aubergines and courgettes in batches until charred on both sides. Transfer to the pan of tomatoes, cover and simmer for 5–10 minutes, until softened.

Divide among 6 individual ovenproof dishes, or one large dish. Cool, then cover and chill.

45 MINUTES AHEAD:

Preheat the oven to 180°C/350°F/Gas mark 4. Put the vegetables in the oven and bake for 15 minutes.

Remove from the oven and make 6 wells for the eggs, then break an egg into each dish and season with salt and pepper. Return to the oven for 15 minutes, until the eggs have set.

DINNERTIME:

Serve the spiced vegetables with their wobbly baked eggs, a dollop of yogurt, chopped parsley and some warm flatbread.

TART: For a non-veggie, moussaka-ish version, add lamb mince to the onions before the tomatoes.

TWEAK: Instead of eggs, dot the top with feta or manouri cheese and bake until soft.

TOMORROW: This will make a great breakfast, a sort of Middle Eastern *huevos rancheros*.

SPICE-ROASTED CARROTS WITH PANEER AND SESAME

SERVES 4–6

1 tbsp coriander seeds

1 tsp cumin seeds

2 tbsp sesame seeds

1 tsp black onion seeds
(kalonji or nigella)

1 tbsp runny honey

4 tbsp groundnut (peanut) oil

1kg/2¼lb carrots, peeled and
sliced thickly at an angle

2 red onions, peeled
and sliced

2 green chillies, deseeded
and sliced

salt and pepper

200g/7oz paneer, cubed

a good handful of fresh
coriander (cilantro)

For the dressing

juice of ½ lemon

2 tbsp groundnut (peanut) oil

a few shakes of toasted
sesame oil

This dish can be served hot or at room temperature, and indeed as a side dish to a curry. Nonetheless it works well as a main course in its own right, and needs only some steamed rice or warm flatbread and perhaps a little raita alongside.

UP TO 2 DAYS AHEAD:

Preheat the oven to 220°C/425°F/Gas mark 7.

Put a dry frying pan over a medium heat and add the coriander seeds and cumin seeds. Toast for a minute, shuggling the pan now and then to prevent burning, then roughly crush. Following the same method, toast the sesame and onion seeds. Mix all this together with the honey and oil, and coat the carrots, onions and chillies with the mixture, seasoning with salt and pepper as you do so.

Tip the vegetables into a roasting pan and roast for 40 minutes, shaking occasionally. Cool, cover and chill.

1 HOUR AHEAD:

Preheat the oven to 140°C/275°F/Gas mark 1, and warm the carrots through.

30 MINUTES AHEAD:

Make the dressing by mixing the lemon juice, groundnut oil and sesame oil. Season with salt and pepper to taste.

Heat a little oil in a non-stick frying pan over a medium-high heat and cook the paneer until crisp and golden. Add to the carrots, stir through and keep warm.

DINNERTIME:

Toss the carrots with the dressing, then scatter with a good handful of coriander leaves and serve.

TART: Add a handful of cooked chickpeas to the carrots.
TWEAK: Omit the chillies if you prefer something milder.
TOMORROW: This is good fridge buffet food – just what you want to find should you get back late from 'work'.

RED HERRING WITH LOVAGE AND PARSLEY SAUCE

SERVES 6

500g/1lb 2oz beetroot

300ml/10fl oz/1¼ cups white wine vinegar

250g/9oz/1¼ cups caster (superfine) sugar

2 shallots, peeled and finely sliced

a bunch of dill, finely chopped – reserve a few fronds to garnish

6 herring, cleaned, boned and butterflied – the fishmonger can do this

For the lovage and parsley sauce

25g/1oz lovage, leaves only

25g/1oz parsley, leaves only

1 tbsp capers

1 garlic clove, peeled and crushed to a paste

juice of 1 lemon

100ml/3½fl oz/7 tbsp olive oil

salt and pepper

When a magician performed at the Secret Larder, I was unable to resist creating a menu of half-baked puns and magical allusions. Hence the rabbit in a hat (p.75) and flowers up a sleeve (p.86). Nonetheless the dishes all hung together pretty well, and this was a particular hit, with flavours that rubbed along like old friends. The beetroot pickling juice adds a lovely sweet and sour contrast, while there is something both fresh and somehow addictive about lovage. (If you can't find lovage, then a good handful of celery leaves will do the trick.)

You will need to pickle the beetroot a day or two ahead. The sauce should be made on the day you want to serve it, but the herring itself cooks in a flash. Serve with flageolet bean salad (p.172) or potato salad (p.152), omitting the lovage.

UP TO 2 DAYS AHEAD:

Put the beetroot in a pan of salted water and bring to a boil. Simmer for about 40 minutes, or until easily pierced with a skewer. Drain and leave to cool. When cool, rub with your thumb to remove the skins. Thinly slice the beetroot.

Stir the vinegar and sugar in a saucepan over a low heat until the sugar has dissolved, then add the shallots and bring to a boil. Simmer for 3 minutes, then pour over the beetroot. Add the dill, cover and leave until cool.

UP TO 4 HOURS AHEAD:

To make the sauce, bring a pan of salted water to a boil. Fill a bowl with iced water. Introduce the lovage and parsley to the hot water for no more than 10 seconds, then plunge them straight into the iced water. Leave for a minute or so, until cold, then remove and press out any excess water. Blend or finely chop with the capers, garlic and lemon juice, then slowly stir or blend in the olive oil. Season with salt and pepper to taste and set aside.

10–15 MINUTES AHEAD:

Drain the beetroot, tipping the pickling juice into a wide saucepan or sauté pan. Bring this to a boil and gently slide in the herring. Reduce the heat and poach for 4–5 minutes.

DINNERTIME:
Serve the red herring with the pickled beetroot and the lovage and parsley sauce.

TART: I like the relative simplicity of the sauce, though you could make it more of a salsa-verde-type affair by adding anchovy and a little mustard.

TWEAK: Do play around with herbs, adding things like mint, rosemary and tarragon to the sauce. Should herring prove hard to track down, use mackerel as an alternative.

TOMORROW: Toss any leftover beetroot and herb sauce through a salad with some smoked mackerel.

FISH STEW WITH ROUILLE

SERVES 6–8

olive oil

2 onions, peeled and
finely chopped

2 sticks of celery,
finely chopped

2 garlic cloves, peeled and
finely chopped

1 fennel bulb, trimmed and
finely chopped

salt and pepper

2 tsp fennel seeds, crushed

1 dried red chilli

1 piece of orange peel

150ml/5fl oz/⅔ cup dry
vermouth or white wine

1kg/2¼lb cherry tomatoes,
or 2 x 400g/14oz cans
tomatoes

1 bay leaf

500g/1lb 2oz squid, cleaned
and sliced into rings

500g/1lb 2oz white fish,
such as bream, cod or
pollack, skinned and cut
into chunks

500g/1lb 2oz mussels,
cleaned, any open or
broken ones discarded

100g/3½oz/1 cup ground
almonds

For the rouille

1 red pepper

1 garlic clove, peeled
and crushed

3–4 saffron strands

2 tbsp fresh breadcrumbs

100ml/3½fl oz/7 tbsp olive oil

A good fish stew is one of the more glorious things to plonk in front of somebody. When the fish is fresh, the shellfish gleaming, and the air thick with fennel and tomato and garlic, all seems well in the world. Permutations are many, and so I suppose this recipe hails from everywhere and nowhere, though I think the addition of ground almonds to thicken is a particularly Spanish twist.

Rouille is a red pepper and oil-based sauce that can be made a day ahead, as can the aromatic tomato base for the stew. You'll also want to clean your squid and mussels a few hours before dinner and put them back in the fridge.

You could serve this quite happily with naught but some crusty bread. Spring greens (p.167) would be a healthy side dish.

UP TO A DAY AHEAD:

To make the rouille, roast the pepper over a direct flame or in a hot oven (220°C/425°F/Gas mark 7) until blistered all over and softened. Put in a bowl and cover with clingfilm for 10 minutes – this helps the skin come off – then peel and deseed. Roughly chop, then whiz in a blender with the garlic, saffron and bread-crumbs. With the blender running, slowly pour in the oil. Season with salt and pepper to taste and set aside until needed.

Heat a little oil in a large saucepan over a low heat. Add the onions, celery, garlic and fennel. Season with salt and pepper, cover and cook for 15 minutes, until softened. Add the fennel seeds, chilli and orange peel, and stir over a high heat for a minute or so before tipping in the booze. Simmer for a minute, then add the tomatoes and bay leaf, cover and cook over a low heat for 20 minutes. Leave to cool, then cover and chill.

45 MINUTES AHEAD:

If necessary, reheat the tomato mixture, then add the squid, cover and gently simmer.

30 MINUTES AHEAD:

Sprinkle a little salt over the white fish and toss thoroughly. This extracts moisture and creates a firmer texture.

10 MINUTES AHEAD:

Add the fish, mussels and almonds to the pan. Stir well, cover and continue to simmer gently.

DINNERTIME:

Taste the stew for seasoning and add a pinch of salt if necessary. Serve with a spoonful of rouille on top.

BAKED SEA BREAM IN A BAG

SERVES 6

olive oil

6 spring onions (scallions), trimmed and halved vertically

2 courgettes (zucchini), thinly sliced

2 fennel bulbs, trimmed and thinly sliced

salt and pepper

6 sprigs of thyme

6 sprigs of tarragon

1 lemon, sliced

6 sea bream, gutted and descaled

The idea behind cooking in a bag – or *en papillote* as the French, and indeed many British people, have it – is to let the fish gently steam in the aromas of all the other ingredients while its own juices are locked in for good measure. It's a rather more restful way of cooking fish than, say, frying, and creates something of a one-pot dish. All you need is a few new potatoes and perhaps a green salad, or the potato salad with anchovy and lovage (p.152).

You'll need 12 pieces of foil to make the bags, which you can pack several hours ahead of the dinner.

UP TO 6 HOURS AHEAD:

Heat a little oil in a ridged griddle or frying pan and, in batches, char the spring onions, courgettes and fennel on both sides, seasoning with salt and pepper as you go, until blistered and smoky. Cool.

Take a sheet of foil and lay on top a couple of pieces of spring onion, a few slices of courgette and some fennel. Tuck a sprig of thyme and tarragon and a slice of lemon inside one of the fish and lay it on top of the vegetables. Place another sheet of foil on top and fold at three of the edges to seal, leaving one side open. Repeat with the other fish and then chill.

45 MINUTES AHEAD:

Remove the fish from the fridge. Throw salt, pepper and a good glug of olive oil into each bag. Now fold the final side and seal thoroughly. Preheat the oven to 200°C/400°F/Gas mark 6.

20 MINUTES AHEAD:

Bake the fish parcels for 20 minutes.

DINNERTIME:

Put the foil bags on plates and serve.

TART: There's pretty much a carte blanche as to what vegetables you put in here, though if adding, say, potatoes, you'll want to boil them first. Try leeks or carrots, cut into matchsticks (you won't need to griddle these).

TWEAK: I often do this with more of an Asian angle – try leaving out the fennel and courgette and instead adding ginger, chillies, lime juice, lemongrass and fish sauce with a few baby pak choi. Instead of the bream, use pieces of salmon fillet.

ROAST STUFFED MACKEREL
WITH LENTILS AND BACON

SERVES 6

olive oil

50g/1¾oz/½ cup dried
   breadcrumbs

2 shallots, peeled and
   finely chopped

2 garlic cloves, peeled and
   crushed to a paste

1 red chilli, deseeded and
   finely chopped

10 anchovy fillets, chopped

a big bunch of parsley,
   finely chopped

1 tsp finely chopped rosemary

zest of 1 lemon

salt and pepper

6 spankingly fresh mackerel,
   about 300g/10½oz each,
   whole and not cleaned

For the lentils

1 onion, peeled and
   finely chopped

1 stick of celery,
   finely chopped

100g/3½oz smoked streaky
   bacon, finely chopped

300g/10½oz/1½ cups green or
   Puy lentils, rinsed

600ml/20fl oz/2½ cups chicken
   or vegetable stock

To serve

salsa verde (p.128)

This method requires either a certain level of deftness with a sharp knife or a friendly relationship with a fishmonger. Boning and stuffing the fish is something to get out of the way long before your guests appear; it's fiddly but not too challenging.

You can if you wish just stuff the cavity of the cleaned but unboned fish, though that means when it comes to eating you have to work your way around the bones as opposed to hacking straight through a cross section of meat and stuffing. Otherwise, you can take two mackerel fillets and put the stuffing in between before wrapping in bacon or prosciutto.

Serve with salsa verde (p.128) and braised lettuce (p.179).

UP TO 2 DAYS AHEAD:

Heat a little oil in a frying pan and add the breadcrumbs. Cook, stirring occasionally, until golden, then remove and set aside. Add a splash more oil and gently cook the shallots until softened – about 10 minutes – then throw in the garlic, chilli, anchovies, parsley, rosemary and lemon zest. Season with a good pinch of salt and plenty of pepper, and cook for a further minute or so, then mix with the breadcrumbs. Cover and chill.

UP TO 6 HOURS AHEAD:

Using a sharp knife, chop off the heads of your fish. Now, instead of cutting along the belly as you normally would to gut a fish, carefully cut down either side of the spine to separate the flesh and the bone – make sure you don't cut through the belly (see photograph on p.114). Pull out the bones and guts and clean the fish, checking for and tweezing out any stray bones. You now have a boned and butterflied mackerel. (If you don't feel up to this process, I'm sure a fishmonger would be happy to do it for you, but it is remarkably straightforward and surprisingly fun.)

Pat the fish dry and fill each cavity with the cold stuffing, then roll each fish tightly in clingfilm and chill.

1 HOUR AHEAD:

Remove the fish from the fridge. Preheat the oven to 200°C/400°F/ Gas mark 6.

For the lentils, heat a little olive oil in a large-ish saucepan and gently cook the onion and celery until softened. Add the bacon and fry for a couple of minutes, stirring regularly, then add the lentils and stock. Bring to a boil, cover and simmer gently for 20 minutes, then take off the heat. *[method continues on p.114]*

20 MINUTES AHEAD:
Unwrap the mackerel and put them in a roasting pan. Rub with a little oil and a good pinch of salt and roast for 15 minutes.

DINNERTIME:
Serve the mackerel with the lentils and salsa verde.

TART: Wrap the mackerel in prosciutto and fry for a couple of minutes to crisp up before roasting for 10 minutes.

TWEAK: Aside from the tweaks mentioned in the intro, you could omit the lentils in favour of something lighter – say, couscous in the summertime – or try a different stuffing, such as one with pine nuts, raisins and cooked spinach.

TOMORROW: Leftover lentils are lovely tossed through a salad.

POACHED SEA TROUT WITH HOLLANDAISE

SERVES 6

1.2kg/2lb 12oz sea trout fillets, cut into 6 more or less equal-sized pieces

For the poaching liquid

150ml/5fl oz/⅔ cup dry white wine

1 carrot

1 stick of celery

½ onion, peeled

1 tsp peppercorns

1 tbsp salt

1 bay leaf

a sprig of thyme

For the hollandaise

250g/9oz/generous 1 cup butter

2 egg yolks

juice of 1 lemon

salt

a pinch of cayenne pepper

Such a beautiful fish, sea trout. Its arrival in early spring always seems to be one of the first signs that the winter is over, particularly because it's a time of year when there's so little happening on the fruit and veg front.

The fish can be served cold, cooked a day ahead and kept chilled. The last-minute thing here is the hollandaise sauce, which is entirely worth it. Serve with buttered samphire with garlic (p.176).

UP TO A DAY AHEAD:

Put all the ingredients for the poaching liquid in a large saucepan and top up with 2 litres/3½ pints/2 quarts water. Bring to a boil and simmer for 30 minutes. Drop in the fish, then take the pan off the heat. Leave for 10 minutes, then remove the trout. Leave to cool, then cover and chill.

1 HOUR AHEAD:

Take the fish out of the fridge.

30 MINUTES AHEAD:

To make the hollandaise, gently melt the butter and set aside.

Bring a small pan of water to a boil and then put over the lowest possible heat. Sit a heatproof bowl on top, making sure it doesn't touch the water. Add the egg yolks and whisk vigorously until they become pale and start to streak the side of the bowl. Take off the heat and, ever so slowly – starting with a drop at a time – add the melted butter, whisking as you go. Continue whisking and pouring in a slow, steady stream. If it looks like it's going to curdle, add a splash of cold water. Once all the butter has been incorporated and the hollandaise is thick and glossy, whisk in the lemon juice and season with salt and a pinch of cayenne.

DINNERTIME:

Serve the sea trout with a generous dollop of hollandaise.

TWEAK: Substitute salmon for sea trout if necessary. If you have a fish kettle, use a gutted 1.5kg/3lb 5oz fish instead of the fillets: put all the ingredients into it cold; fill with water, bring to a boil, cover and turn off the heat. Leave until cool then remove, skin, and serve at leisure.

TOMORROW: Mix leftover sea trout with mashed potatoes and lots of chopped herbs and form into fish cakes – cook in hot oil for a few minutes on each side and serve with peas.

A FIERY PRAWN CURRY WITH A FRESH YOGURT AND HERB SAUCE

SERVES 4–6

2 fresh red chillies,
    stalks removed
2 garlic cloves, peeled and
    roughly chopped
1 small shallot, peeled and
    roughly chopped
a small knob of fresh ginger,
    roughly chopped
juice of 1 lime
1 tbsp vegetable oil
2 tsp black mustard seeds
20 curry leaves (fresh if
    possible, dried otherwise)
1 dried red chilli
a pinch of asafoetida
    (optional)
1 tsp turmeric
1 tbsp coriander seeds,
    roughly crushed
1 tsp cumin seeds, crushed
200ml/7fl oz/generous ¾ cup
    coconut cream
200ml/7fl oz/generous ¾ cup
    fish stock
salt
1kg/2¼lb jumbo prawns
    (shrimp), peeled
    or unpeeled
200g/7oz mangetout (snow
    peas), sliced once or
    twice vertically
a small handful of fresh
    coriander (cilantro) leaves
For the yogurt and herb sauce
250g/9oz/1 cup plain yogurt
juice of 1 lime
a big handful of fresh
    coriander (cilantro) leaves
a small handful of mint leaves

We Brits love a good curry, and as do-ahead cookery goes it's always a winner, improving in flavour over a couple of days. Serve with rice and/or warm naan or roti bread.

I favour unpeeled jumbo prawns, as I enjoy the crunch and the flavour from the shell and the head, though if you prefer use peeled prawns, or compromise with half and half.

UP TO 2 DAYS AHEAD:
Put the chillies, garlic, shallot, ginger and lime juice in a blender with a couple of tablespoons of water and blend until smooth. Alternatively use a pestle and mortar.

Heat the oil in a wok or sauté pan over a medium heat and add the mustard seeds. When these start to pop, throw in the curry leaves, dried chilli, asafoetida, turmeric and coriander and cumin seeds, and prod around the pan for a couple of minutes, taking care not to burn. Stir in the paste you made earlier and then add the coconut cream and fish stock. Season with a good pinch of salt and simmer for about 20 minutes, until reduced by half. Cool, cover and chill.

UP TO 2 HOURS AHEAD:
To make the yogurt and herb sauce, put all the ingredients in a blender and whiz. Alternatively, finely chop the herbs and mix with the yogurt and lime juice. Season with a pinch of salt, cover and chill.

15–20 MINUTES AHEAD:
Put the curry base over a medium heat and bring to a gentle boil. Add the prawns and simmer for 3 minutes. Stir in the mangetout and simmer for a further 1–2 minutes.

DINNERTIME:
Scatter the curry with a few coriander leaves and serve with the yogurt sauce.

TART: As a last-minute flourish, heat 2–3cm/about 1in of oil over a high heat and throw in some finely sliced shallots. Fry for 30–60 seconds until crisp, then drain on kitchen paper, before scattering over the curry.
TWEAK: Use a mixture of fish, such as monkfish, cod and prawns.
TOMORROW: Leftover curry beats a bowl of bran flakes for breakfast, doesn't it?

BRAISED PIG CHEEK WITH POLENTA AND GREMOLATA

SERVES 6

325g/11½oz/generous 1 cup
    salt (optional)
12–15 pig cheeks, about
    1.2kg/2lb 12oz total weight
2 tbsp plain (all-purpose) flour
salt and pepper
olive oil
1 onion, peeled and
    finely chopped
1 stick of celery,
    finely chopped
2 garlic cloves, peeled
    and finely sliced
½ bottle of red wine
2 tbsp tomato purée
    (tomato paste)
300ml/10fl oz/1¼ cups water

For the polenta
1.2 litres/2 pints/5 cups water
300g/10½oz/2½ cups polenta
    (cornmeal)
50g/1¾oz/4 tbsp butter

For the gremolata
a good handful of
    flat-leaf parsley
zest of 1 lemon
1 garlic clove, peeled and
    very finely chopped

TART: To further Italify this dish, add some black olives as you put the cheeks in the oven.

TWEAK: Cook the polenta in advance, leaving out the butter; when cooked, tip it onto an oiled baking sheet and leave to cool. To serve, cut into slices and fry until crisp.

TOMORROW: Shred leftover pig cheek and serve as a pig cheek ragù with pasta.

I love serving pig cheeks to friends. They have invariably never tried them before, and react with a certain amount of trepidation at the prospect of eating Babe's jowls before surrendering to their soft, piggy perfection. Supermarkets seem to be stocking them increasingly, though no doubt a butcher would be delighted to get some in for you.

Serve with spring greens (p.167), omitting lemon and garlic.

UP TO 2 DAYS AHEAD (OPTIONAL):

Mix the salt with 4 litres water, stir until dissolved, then brine the pig cheeks in this solution for 24 hours. Soak in fresh water for 1 hour, changing the water every 15 minutes, then pat dry. This ensures the meat is well seasoned throughout and good and juicy.

UP TO A DAY AHEAD:

Dry the cheeks thoroughly, then toss them in the flour along with a pinch of salt and pepper. Heat a little oil in a frying pan over a high heat and brown the cheeks all over in batches. Remove to a large ovenproof pan.

Add a little more oil to the frying pan if necessary, and over a medium heat soften the onion, celery and garlic, stirring regularly. Add to the cheeks. Deglaze the frying pan with a slosh of red wine and stir to dislodge any bits of caramelized pig, then add this all to the ovenproof pan, along with the rest of the wine, tomato purée and water. Bring to a simmer, cover and cook over a low heat for 2 hours, or in the oven at 160°C/325°F/Gas mark 3. Chill overnight or keep warm until dinner.

To make the gremolata, finely chop the parsley and mix with the lemon zest and garlic.

1 HOUR BEFORE DINNER:

Gently reheat the braised pig cheeks over a low heat if necessary, stirring occasionally. Taste for seasoning.

For the polenta, bring the water to a boil with a good pinch of salt and slowly pour in the polenta, whisking continuously to avoid lumps. Wear your sleeves pulled down – this stuff spits. Turn the heat right down and cook for 45 minutes to 1 hour, stirring occasionally. If the polenta looks too dry, just add a splash of hot water. Beat in the butter and a twist of pepper.

DINNERTIME:

Taste the polenta for seasoning and add a pinch more salt if necessary. Serve with the pig cheeks and a sprinkling of gremolata.

HAM HOCK WITH PEARL BARLEY AND A BEETROOT SALAD

SERVES 6

2–3 unsmoked ham hocks,
    about 2kg/4½lb total
    weight
2 onions, peeled and
    roughly chopped
4 sticks of celery,
    roughly chopped
2–3 garlic cloves, peeled
    and squashed with the
    flat of a knife
1 carrot, snapped in half
1 bay leaf
a few peppercorns
1 x 500ml bottle of dry cider
For the pearl barley
300g/10½oz/1½ cups pearl
    barley
1 tbsp tarragon,
    finely chopped
For the beetroot and
parsley salad
500g/1lb 2oz cooked beetroot
1 tsp Dijon mustard
1 tbsp white wine vinegar
2 tbsp olive oil
salt and pepper
100g/3½oz parsley, leaves only

TOMORROW: Finely shred any leftover meat and mix through with a good handful of chopped herbs and, if you have any left, the beetroot and parsley. Line a small loaf tin or bowl with clingfilm and press in the meat. Pour over a good few spoonfuls of the cooking liquor, cover and refrigerate overnight with something heavy on top. Turn out and serve the terrine with toast and butter.

This was the first main course I ever served at the supper club, a dish I remember fondly despite the butterflies associated with it. That night I took 'do-ahead dinners' to excessive lengths – I laid the tables two days in advance, polishing cutlery and glasses, checking and rechecking salt cellars and pepper grinders, and chopping, peeling and cooking as much as I could. The evening went off without a hitch and this dish was a great success.

If you prefer, you could serve the ham hocks with dauphinois potatoes (p.153) instead of the pearl barley.

UP TO 2 DAYS AHEAD:

Put the ham hocks in a large saucepan, cover with cold water and bring slowly to a boil. Drain and rinse the hocks. This gets rid of any excess salt. Return to the pan along with the rest of the ingredients. Cover with water and bring back to a boil. Simmer for 3–4 hours over a low heat, skimming off any scum as and when necessary. When the meat is soft and falling off the bone, take it out of the liquid and leave to rest for 10 minutes. Skin the hocks, discard the skin and bone, and roughly shred the meat, using a couple of forks. Stir a few spoonfuls of the cooking liquor through the shredded ham, cover and chill, or keep warm until dinner. Set aside 900ml/generous 1½ pints/3½ cups of the ham stock for the pearl barley, refrigerate or freeze the rest for future soups.

UP TO 6 HOURS AHEAD:

To make the beetroot and parsley salad, chop the beetroot into cubes and set aside. Whisk together the mustard, vinegar and oil and season with salt and pepper. Cover and set aside.

1 HOUR AHEAD:

Rinse the pearl barley under running water, then put it in a large pan with the ham stock. Bring to a boil and simmer over a medium-low heat for 45 minutes, until the barley is tender and has absorbed all the liquid. Season with salt and pepper and stir through the tarragon.

If necessary, put the ham over a low heat and warm through.

DINNERTIME:

Toss the beetroot cubes and parsley leaves with the dressing. Serve the ham hocks with the pearl barley, beetroot and parsley salad and a pot of mustard.

STUFFED CABBAGE (*GOLUBTSY*)

SERVES 4–6

olive oil

1 onion, peeled and
    finely chopped

1 stick of celery,
    finely chopped

salt and pepper

2 garlic cloves, peeled
    and finely chopped

2 tsp ground coriander

400g/14oz minced
    (ground) beef

100g/3½oz minced
    (ground) pork

200g/7oz/1 cup pearl barley

800ml/scant 1½ pints/
    generous 3¼ cups chicken
    or beef stock

2 tbsp tomato purée
    (tomato paste)

1 bay leaf

1 large white cabbage

20g/¾oz/1½ tbsp butter

300g/10½oz passata
    (strained tomatoes)

150ml/5fl oz/⅔ cup sour
    cream

1 tsp paprika

sugar

This recipe comes via two Russian friends, Serge and Karine. If that sounds like an excuse then it shouldn't. Russian food is delicious, hearty, frugal and generous – the sort of fare you need to keep you going through the winter, and by no means only edible with considerable amounts of vodka. Though, when in Rome…

UP TO 2 DAYS AHEAD:

Heat a little oil in a large pan over a low heat and add the onion and celery. Season with salt and pepper and cook gently for 10–12 minutes, until softened. Add the garlic and coriander, and stir briefly before adding the beef and pork and whacking up the heat. Stir for a couple of minutes until the meat is coloured, then add the pearl barley, stock, tomato purée and bay leaf. Bring to a boil and simmer gently for 1 hour, adding a little hot water if it looks dry. Taste for seasoning, then cool, cover and chill.

UP TO A DAY AHEAD:

Carefully remove the core from the cabbage with a sharp knife. Bring a large pan of water to a boil and add the cabbage. Simmer for 5 minutes, then remove and run under cold water. Peel off the outer leaves until you have 8–12 large leaves (depending on how many you're feeding). Cut out and discard any tough veins from each leaf and pat dry.

Put a good spoonful of the mince and barley on the under-side of each cabbage leaf and wrap into a sausage shape, then line up in an ovenproof dish.

Melt the butter in a small saucepan and add the passata and sour cream. Season with salt and pepper, paprika and a pinch of sugar, and very gently simmer for 15 minutes. Leave to cool, then pour over the stuffed cabbage. Refrigerate or continue.

1 HOUR AHEAD:

Preheat the oven to 180°C/350°F/Gas mark 4. Bake the *golubtsy* for 45 minutes.

DINNERTIME:

Serve with something suitably Russian, such as a beetroot and dill salad and boiled potatoes.

TWEAK: If you're not a fan of pearl barley, use rice instead, though this will need less cooking. An odd Turkmen twist is to use green tea instead of stock.

TOMORROW: The *golubtsy* will keep for a couple of days in the fridge.

SOUTHERN-STYLE SHOULDER OF PORK

SERVES 6–8

1 small shoulder of pork,
   weighing 3–4kg/6½–9lb
2 garlic cloves, peeled and
   crushed to a paste
2 tsp finely chopped rosemary
a big handful of parsley,
   finely chopped
2 tsp fine salt
1 tbsp hot smoked paprika
1 tbsp fennel seeds, crushed
2 tsp cayenne pepper
100ml/3½fl oz/7 tbsp olive oil
250g/9oz fine hickory chips
   (optional)

For the barbecue sauce
olive oil
1 onion, peeled and
   finely chopped
4 garlic cloves, peeled and
   crushed to a paste
4 red chillies, deseeded and
   roughly chopped
2 tsp cumin seeds, crushed
1 tbsp coriander seeds,
   crushed
1 tbsp hot smoked paprika
½ tsp ground cloves
zest of ½ orange
100ml/3½fl oz/6–7 tbsp
   bourbon (optional)
700g/1lb 9oz passata
   (strained tomatoes)
2 tsp finely chopped
   thyme leaves
1 tsp finely chopped rosemary
3 tbsp red wine vinegar
100g/3½oz/½ cup brown
   sugar
2 tbsp English mustard
1 tbsp liquid smoke (optional)
salt and pepper

Barbecue is taken extremely seriously in the US. Across the southern states acres of farmland are overrun each year by competing teams of dungareed fire fanatics, who spend entire days slowly smoking pieces of meat large enough to club a hippopotamus to death with. There is a great deal of ritual, and much nerdy obsession over what is right and what is wrong. This recipe is 'wrong' off the bat, because it uses an oven, but as a bastardization of the real thing, it's not so far off the mark.

It's all about the smoke, which, if you don't have a barbecue – or if you live in the UK and it's raining – is hard to create. Or is it? Hickory chips are easy to come by in garden centres or online, and liquid smoke – the not-so-secret ingredient to this barbecue sauce – is also available via the internet. If using the hickory chips, you'll also need a roasting pan with a trivet.

The barbecue sauce will improve over time, so make this well ahead if you need to. The slow-roasted pork will happily wait while you finish putting together the rest of dinner.

Serve with Boston baked beans (p.170), some soft buns and a crunchy salad.

UP TO A WEEK AHEAD:

To make the barbecue sauce, heat a little oil in a large saucepan over a low heat and gently soften the onion. Add the garlic, chillies and spices, and stir over a medium heat for a minute or so, then add all the remaining ingredients. Season enthusiastically with salt and pepper, and simmer over a medium heat for 30 minutes, stirring occasionally.

Whiz in a blender until smooth and pass through a sieve back into the pan. Simmer for another 30 minutes, until thickened. Taste for seasoning, and leave to cool. Store in the fridge in sterilized jars (see note on p.2).

UP TO 3 DAYS AHEAD:

Using a sharp knife, score the pork skin all over. Mix all the remaining ingredients – but not the hickory chips – and rub them generously over the pork shoulder. Cover and refrigerate.

10–12 HOURS AHEAD:

Take the pork shoulder out of the fridge.

To smoke the pork (optional): line a roasting pan with foil and tip in the hickory chips. Place over a medium heat until it starts to smoke. Put a trivet over the chips and sit the pork on that, then

cover tightly with a layer of baking parchment and several layers of foil. Leave to smoke over a medium-low heat for 20 minutes.

Preheat the oven to 160°C/325°F/Gas mark 3.

Put the covered shoulder in the oven and roast for 7–8 hours. Whack up the heat to 220°C/425°F/Gas mark 7, remove the foil and parchment, and roast for a further 45 minutes to 1 hour until crisp.

Remove and leave to rest. Gently warm the barbecue sauce through if you fancy.

DINNERTIME:

Separate the crisp skin and set aside. Pull apart the meat with a pair of tongs and serve with barbecue sauce and a piece of crisp skin.

TWEAK: For ease of cooking and shopping, both the hickory chips and liquid smoke can be omitted.
TOMORROW: Leftover pork shoulder – where to begin? Burritos, carnitas, chilli con carne, pulled pork sandwiches with coleslaw… the list goes on.

SLOW-ROASTED PORK BELLY WITH SALSA VERDE

SERVES 4–6

2kg/4½lb pork belly

salt and pepper

2 onions, peeled and
finely sliced

a handful of rosemary
and thyme

200ml/7fl oz/generous ¾ cup
dry cider or white wine

300ml/10fl oz/1¼ cups chicken
stock or water

For the salsa verde

a big handful of parsley leaves

1 tsp finely chopped rosemary

a small handful of mint leaves

1 garlic clove, peeled and
roughly chopped

2 tbsp capers

12 anchovy fillets

1 tbsp Dijon mustard

juice of 1 lemon

100ml/3½fl oz/7 tbsp olive oil

TART: The relative simplicity
of this dish works in its favour,
though you could make it a
one-pot dish by slicing some
new potatoes, cooking them
under the pork with the onions.
TWEAK: Remove the skin
before cooking and score.
Cook the meat separately,
as above, but adding 500ml
dry cider at the beginning of
cooking. While the meat rests,
roast the skin at 220°C/425°F/
Gas mark 7 until crisp.
TOMORROW: Slice leftover
pork belly and toss in Chinese
five-spice, soy sauce and a
little oil. Fry until crisp. Serve
with pak choi and noodles.

Pork belly has become something of a *sine qua non* of pub
menus, and for good reason – it's cheap, simple to cook, versatile
and delicious. Being quite a tough, fatty cut, it responds best to
long, slow cooking, giving the fat a chance to render and the
meat a chance to soften. You are left with one of the most luscious
pieces of meat imaginable. And the oven's done all the work.
Serve with braised shallots (p.162) or spring greens (p.167).

UP TO A DAY AHEAD:

Make the salsa verde by thoroughly blending or finely chopping
all of the ingredients apart from the olive oil. Slowly stir or blend
in the oil and season with pepper. Taste and add a little salt if
necessary. Cover and chill.

4½ HOURS AHEAD:

Using a very sharp knife – I use a scalpel – score the meat at 1cm/
½in intervals. Scatter some salt over the skin and leave for 1 hour.
This draws out excess moisture and gives you crisper crackling.
Preheat the oven to 220°C/425°F/Gas mark 7.

3½ HOURS AHEAD:

Pat the pig skin dry and shake off any excess salt. Pile the onions
and herbs in a roasting pan and lay the pork belly on top. Try not
to leave any stray pieces of onion poking out from under the pork,
as these have a tendency to burn.
Roast the pork in the oven for 20 minutes, then turn the oven
down to 160°C/325°F/Gas mark 3 and roast for a further 2½ hours.

30 MINUTES AHEAD:

Remove the pork and transfer to a carving board to rest. If at this
point the crackling isn't as crisp as you'd like, put the pork in a
different roasting pan and back in the oven at 220°C/425°F/Gas
mark 7 until crisp.
Tip away the excess fat from the original roasting pan, then
put the pan over a high heat. Add the cider or wine and simmer
for a minute or so, scraping up all the pan juices, then add the
stock or water and simmer for 10 minutes. Taste for seasoning and
add a little salt and pepper if necessary.
If you've been crisping up the crackling, rest the pork belly for
5–10 minutes before serving.

DINNERTIME:

Carve the pork and crackling into nice thick chunks, and serve
with a spoonful of the gravy and a good dollop of salsa verde.

NECK OF LAMB WITH ROASTED GARLIC AND FLAGEOLET BEANS

SERVES 6

6 lamb neck fillets
350ml/12fl oz/1½ cups red
   wine
1 onion, peeled and sliced
2 garlic cloves, peeled and
   lightly crushed
a few peppercorns, crushed
1 bay leaf
a sprig of rosemary
1 tbsp fine salt
6 garlic bulbs
salt and pepper
olive oil

For the beans

2 shallots, peeled and
   finely chopped
1 garlic clove, peeled and
   crushed to a paste
400g/14oz dried flageolet
   beans, soaked overnight,
   or 2 x 400g/14oz cans
a bunch of parsley,
   finely chopped
juice of ½ lemon

TART: For something that is more stew-like, add a can of chopped tomatoes and some chopped black olives to the lamb when you put it in the roasting pan with the marinade.

TWEAK: Serve with mashed potatoes instead of beans for a more wintery incarnation.

TOMORROW: Leftover lamb will freeze well, or slice and grill it before putting in a wrap.

Lamb neck is certainly not something I remember eating as a child, though it now seems to be an increasingly popular cut of meat. For clarification as to where exactly it comes from, you need only pinch the muscle that runs from the back of your head down to your shoulder.

Serve with braised lettuce with peas and herbs (p.179), or a tomato salad.

UP TO 3 DAYS AHEAD:

Put the lamb in a bowl, tip in the wine and chuck in the onion, garlic cloves, peppercorns, bay, rosemary and salt. Cover and chill. The longer you can leave it to marinate, the better, though a couple of hours is better than nothing.

UP TO A DAY AHEAD:

Preheat the oven to 200°C/400°F/Gas mark 6.

Cut the top third off the garlic bulbs and discard. Drizzle with olive oil and season with salt and pepper, then put cut side down on a baking sheet. Roast for 30 minutes, until soft and lightly golden, then remove.

Meanwhile, pat the meat dry and brown all over in a hot frying pan, with a little oil to help it along. Put in a roasting pan along with the marinade and bring to a boil, then transfer to the oven. Turn the oven down to 160°C/325°F/Gas mark 3 and cook for 2 hours, then cool, cover and chill.

1 HOUR AHEAD:

Preheat the oven to 110°C/225°F/Gas mark ¼ and gently warm the lamb and roasted garlic.

For the beans, heat a little olive oil in a large saucepan and gently cook the shallots and garlic until softened. Add the beans and cover with water. Bring to a boil and simmer for 40 minutes or so, until soft. Canned beans will need only 3–4 minutes. Drain and add the parsley, lemon juice, a good glug of olive oil and plenty of salt and pepper. Cover until ready to serve.

DINNERTIME:

Thickly slice the lamb and serve with the beans, roasted garlic and a spoonful of the lamb cooking juice.

25-MINUTE ROAST LEG OF LAMB
WITH FRESH MINT SAUCE

SERVES 6–8

1 leg of lamb, weighing
    2.5kg/5½lb
a few sprigs of rosemary
2 fat garlic cloves, peeled
    and chopped into
    little matchsticks
a few pieces of shaved
    orange peel, sliced
    into strips
salt and pepper
olive oil

For the sauce

about 85g/3oz mint,
    leaves only
a splash of boiling water
2 tbsp caster (superfine) sugar
3 tbsp white wine vinegar

TART: Peel and halve 3 onions
and arrange around the lamb,
cut side up. Drizzle with oil and
season with salt and pepper
and roast with the lamb.

TOMORROW: Make a pasty:
chop leftover lamb and mix
with a chopped and fried
onion, a chopped and boiled
potato, and a spoonful of
a good chilli sauce. Cut a
rolled sheet of puff pastry into
a round and put the lamb
mixture on one half. Fold over
and pinch round the edge.
Brush with beaten egg and
bake at 180°C/350°F/Gas
mark 4 for 20 minutes.

I didn't believe it myself. When Jim Fisher, head honcho of
cookery school Cook in France, told me he could roast a leg
of lamb in 25 minutes, I said: *'Mais monsieur, ce n'est pas
possible'*. But he assured me otherwise, and indeed showed me
with a proud flourish. It's a brilliant recipe, so thanks, Jim.

At this point I should highlight the fact that, while the lamb is
only roasted for 25 minutes, it needs another 1½ hours to finish,
giving you plenty of time to finish any bits and pieces and spend
time with your guests. Should your leg of lamb be larger or smaller,
you'll need to tweak the time in the oven by about a minute for
every 200g/7oz either way: e.g. a 2.3kg/5lb leg of lamb will need
24 minutes.

Serve with baked onions (p.159) or dauphinois potatoes
(p.153).

6 HOURS AHEAD:

Remove the lamb from the fridge: it is crucial that it's at room
temperature before cooking.

3 HOURS AHEAD:

Using a sharp knife, make about 20 deep incisions in the skin side
of the lamb. Into each hole, stick a few rosemary sprigs, a sliver of
garlic and a piece of orange peel. Season all over with salt and
pepper and a flick of oil.

Preheat the oven to full whack – mine goes up to 250°C/500°F/
Gas mark 10.

2 HOURS AHEAD:

Put the lamb in the oven. Roast for 25 minutes. Remove and cover
tightly with 10 sheets of foil, then top with several thick towels,
coats, or anything that will keep the heat in. Leave for 1½ hours.

Meanwhile, make the mint sauce by blitzing all the ingredients
together in a blender, or finely chopping the mint and mixing. If it's
a little dry, add a splash more water.

DINNERTIME:

Take off the layers of insulation and carve the perfectly pink lamb
into thick slices. Serve with the mint sauce.

STUFFED SHOULDER OF LAMB WITH COCKLES OR CLAMS

SERVES 6–8

1 shoulder of lamb, boned
    and butterflied

olive oil

250g/9oz unsmoked streaky
    bacon, chopped

2 onions, peeled and
    finely chopped

salt and pepper

4 garlic cloves, peeled and
    crushed to a paste

1 tsp chopped thyme leaves

400g/14oz chard, leaves
    stripped from stalks
    and chopped (discard
    the stalks)

500g/1lb 2oz cockles or clams

100ml/3½fl oz/7 tbsp dry
    white wine

a small handful of parsley,
    finely chopped

The union of lamb and seafood – particularly bivalves though also notably anchovies – is one of the most perfect in all of cooking. Lamb's natural sweetness against the salty, ozone tang of a wobbly mollusc makes as much sense as potatoes and cream, or ham and mustard.

Ask your butcher to butterfly the lamb shoulder for you, or buy a ready-boned shoulder from the supermarket. You'll need some kitchen string to tie it up once you've stuffed it. As well as the pictures here on p.135, there are useful videos online if you'd like visual guidance on tying up boned joints of meat, but don't worry if it doesn't look particularly professional, as long as it holds its shape it's fine. It's something that's worth doing well in advance. And while the lamb's in the oven, you've got 2 or 3 hours to organize the rest of your menu.

Serve with courgette gratin (p.178), flageolet bean salad (p.172), or lentils with feta, rocket, chilli and croutons (p.173).

UP TO A DAY AHEAD:

Heat a little oil in a large-ish saucepan, add the bacon and fry until crisp. Add the onions and a good pinch of salt and pepper, cover and cook over a low heat for 10 minutes, until softened. Add the garlic and thyme, stir for a minute, then add the chard. Cover and cook for 8 minutes until fully wilted, then take off the heat and leave to cool.

When the stuffing is completely cooled, lay the lamb shoulder out flat, skin side down. Season the lamb with salt and pepper, then spread with the stuffing and roll up, tying tightly with string. Refrigerate until needed or proceed, skipping the next step.

5 HOURS AHEAD:

Remove the lamb from the fridge: it must be at room temperature before cooking.

3½ HOURS AHEAD:

Preheat the oven to 220°C/425°F/Gas mark 7.

Rub the outside of the lamb with salt, pepper and olive oil, and put in a roasting pan. Cook for 30 minutes, then turn the oven down to 160°C/325°F/Gas mark 3 and roast for a further 2½ hours. Remove from the oven and rest in a warm place.

[method continues on p.134]

1 HOUR AHEAD:

Pick through the cockles or clams and discard any that have broken shells or that remain open after a gentle tap. Put them in a bowl and cover with cold water. Leave for 20 minutes, then lift out the cockles (don't tip them into a colander as this will only chuck the grit back over them).

10 MINUTES AHEAD:

Put a large pan over a medium heat and add a splash of oil. After 30 seconds, throw in the cockles and wine. Cover and leave for 5 minutes, shaking occasionally, until the clams have opened. Toss in the parsley and stir.

DINNERTIME:

Cut the lamb into thick chunks and serve with the cockles and a good spoonful of the cockle cooking liquor.

TART: The stuffing can be oomphed up with the likes of chopped anchovy, black olives and chilli.

TWEAK: If you can't find chard, use spinach or spring greens. This recipe would also work well with a rolled leg of lamb. And, of course, you can omit the cockles/clams if you can't find any.

TOMORROW: Fry a spoonful of ras-el-hanout (a North African spice mix found in most supermarkets these days) in a little oil, and then add slices of the leftover lamb and a small glass of wine. Cover and cook for 20 minutes until soft and warm. Serve with couscous and a dollop of yogurt.

BOURBON-BRAISED BEEF SHORT RIBS

SERVES 6–8

350ml/12fl oz/1½ cups
    bourbon
50g/1¾oz/¼ cup brown sugar
½ onion, peeled and
    finely sliced
1 garlic clove, peeled and
    squashed with the flat
    of a knife
1 tbsp peppercorns, ground
1 tsp chilli flakes
1 tsp dried oregano
2 tsp salt
2 tbsp olive oil
3kg/6½lb beef short ribs
100g/3½oz/6–7 tbsp tomato
    ketchup
a few shakes of Worcestershire
    sauce
1 tbsp English mustard
    powder, mixed with
    1 tbsp water

Unlike a piggy's spare ribs, beef short ribs – or Jacob's ladder – have a substantial amount of meat on them. A gently spiced bourbon bath seems a good way to treat such a handsome ingredient. This is do-ahead cookery at its finest, and like any slow-cooked meat it improves over a day or two.

Serve with baked potatoes.

UP TO 5 DAYS AHEAD:

In a large bowl, stir the bourbon with the sugar until the sugar has dissolved, then add the onion, garlic, pepper, chilli, oregano, salt and olive oil, and give it all a good stir. Cut the short ribs into pieces that will fit in a large pot and add to the marinade. Cover and chill. Turn the ribs in the marinade every now and then.

UP TO 2 DAYS AHEAD:

Preheat the oven to 160°C/325°F/Gas mark 3.

Remove the ribs from the marinade and pat thoroughly dry. Heat a little oil in a frying pan and brown the ribs all over, in batches. Transfer to a large lidded ovenproof pan and pour over the marinade, along with 400ml/14fl oz/scant 1¾ cups water. Bring to a boil, cover and put in the oven for 3 hours.

By now, the meat should come off the bone easily. If not, give it another 30 minutes. Remove from the oven and take the meat out of the liquid. Put the pan over a medium heat and add the ketchup, Worcestershire sauce and mustard. Simmer for 15 minutes until thickened. Meanwhile, pull all the meat off the bones and shred with a fork.

Return the meat to the pan and continue as below, or take the pan off the heat, cool, cover and chill.

1 HOUR AHEAD (IF NECESSARY):

Gently reheat over a low heat, or in the oven at 120°C/250°F/Gas mark ½.

DINNERTIME:

Taste for seasoning and add a little salt or pepper if necessary. Serve.

TART: For added smoke and meat, add fat chunks of smoked bacon to the pan after you've browned the ribs.
TWEAK: This would work with any of the tougher beef cuts – shin, for example – and indeed with pork belly or shoulder.
TOMORROW: Use the leftover meat for rissoles (p.39).

BRAISED SHIN OF BEEF WITH ROASTED BONE MARROW

SERVES 4–6

6 rashers of unsmoked streaky
    bacon, chopped
1.5kg/3lb 5oz beef shin, cut
    into large chunks
2 tbsp plain (all-purpose) flour
salt and pepper
25g/1oz/2 tbsp butter
1 large onion, peeled and
    finely chopped
2 carrots, peeled and
    finely chopped
2 sticks of celery,
    finely chopped
2 garlic cloves, peeled and
    finely sliced
2 tbsp tomato purée
    (tomato paste)
500ml/18fl oz/generous
    2 cups red wine – not your
    cheapest, not your best
1 bay leaf
a sprig of thyme
For the bone marrow
50g/1¾oz/1 cup fresh white
    breadcrumbs
a handful of parsley,
    finely chopped
1 garlic clove, peeled and
    finely chopped
3 x 8cm/3in veal marrow
    bones, split vertically

TWEAK: A few adjustments
transform this into something
totally different. Try adding
ground cumin, smoked
paprika, chilli and kidney beans
for a chunky chilli con carne.
TOMORROW: Warm and
shred leftover meat, top with
mashed potatoes, and bake
for a cottage pie.

Bone marrow might seem like a slightly daunting thing to cook, or indeed find, but on both counts it's fairly straightforward. On the finding front, all you need do is ask the butcher to get some 8cm/3in veal marrow bones for you and, if possible, split them down the middle. The cooking is no more complicated than sticking them in the oven and waiting 15 minutes. So minimal headache for one of the most delicious, rich, unctuous, meaty morsels imaginable. NB bone marrow spoils very quickly so order for the day of serving, but do get your beef braised ahead of time: keeping it in the fridge for a day or two undoubtedly improves it.

Serve with glazed turnips (p.164) or celeriac and horseradish mash (p.161).

UP TO 2 DAYS AHEAD:
Preheat the oven to 160°C/325°F/Gas mark 3.

Heat a little oil in a large ovenproof pan and fry the bacon until crisp. Remove with a slotted spoon. Put the beef and flour in a freezer bag along with a good pinch of salt and a twist of pepper, and give the bag a vigorous shake to coat the meat. In batches, brown the beef all over on a high heat and remove to a bowl for the time being.

Reduce the heat and chuck in the butter, followed shortly by the vegetables and another pinch of salt and pepper. Gently cook, stirring occasionally, until softened – about 15 minutes. Return the meat to the pan along with the tomato purée, wine and herbs. Bring to a boil, cover and pop in the oven for 2–3 hours.

Taste the sauce for seasoning, then cool and chill, or keep warm until dinner.

UP TO 6 HOURS AHEAD:
Combine the breadcrumbs, parsley and garlic for the marrow bones and season with a pinch of salt.

45 MINUTES AHEAD (IF NECESSARY):
Gently warm the stew over a low heat.
Preheat the oven to 200°C/400°F/Gas mark 6.

20 MINUTES AHEAD:
Pile the parsley breadcrumbs on the marrow bones and drizzle with olive oil. Roast for 15 minutes.

DINNERTIME:
Serve the shin and bone with a jar of mustard or horseradish sauce.

CHICKEN PLOV

SERVES 6–8

1.5kg/3lb 5oz chicken thighs

2 tsp fine salt

2 star anise

1 cinnamon stick

½ onion

½ carrot

1 garlic bulb,
    halved horizontally

about 10 peppercorns

For the *plov*

a handful of barberries or
    pomegranate seeds
    (optional)

25g/1oz/2 tbsp butter

2 tbsp olive oil

2 large onions, peeled
    and finely chopped

2 sticks of celery,
    finely chopped

2 garlic cloves, peeled
    and sliced

salt and pepper

2 tsp ground coriander

1 tsp ground cumin

1 tsp paprika

a pinch of saffron strands

a good handful of parsley

400g/14oz/generous 2 cups
    basmati rice

Plov is, supposedly, an Uzbek dish, though in truth its origins are rather more complicated. Like other familiar rice numbers, such as pilau and pilaf, its etymological root is the Farsi *pulaw*. This is why all the way from India and onwards through Central Asia, steamed rice dishes beginning with a 'p' can be found, along with much argument over whose was the original. (I thought, indeed hoped, that with a greater leap the Spanish had landed on the word *paella*, but was informed by Mark Forsyth, author of the brilliant *Etymologicon*, that paella comes from the Spanish for plate.)

Serve with beetroot salad (p.163) or roasted carrots (p.156).

UP TO A DAY AHEAD:

Put the chicken thighs, salt, star anise, cinnamon, onion, carrot, garlic and peppercorns in a large saucepan and cover with water. Bring to a boil, skim off any scum, and gently simmer for 1 hour.

Remove the chicken from the water and leave to rest for 5–10 minutes. Keep the cooking liquor and spices but discard the onion, carrot and garlic; leave to cool, then chill. Using a couple of forks, shred the chicken meat, discarding the skin and bone. Cover and chill.

UP TO 6 HOURS AHEAD:

If using, soak the barberries for 10 minutes in boiling water from the kettle, then drain.

Melt the butter in a large, heavy pan, along with the oil. Add the onions, celery and garlic, and season with salt and pepper. Cook over a low heat for about 15 minutes, stirring occasionally, until softened and slightly golden. Add the spices and cook for a further 2 minutes, stirring regularly. Set aside or continue to the next step.

UP TO 1 HOUR AHEAD:

Take the chicken and the stock out of the fridge. Finely chop the parsley.

Put the rice in a sieve and rinse under cold running water until the water runs clear. This washes off excess starch and ensures perfectly fluffy rice.

30 MINUTES AHEAD:

Put the pan of spicy onion mixture over a medium heat and stir in the rice. Cook for a minute, stirring to make sure all the rice grains are coated with spices and fat, then add 800ml/scant 1½ pints/ generous 3¼ cups of the chicken stock and bring to a boil.

Cover and put over a low heat for 12 minutes. Don't lift the lid. Take off the heat and leave for a further 5 minutes, still without peeking – you need to keep the steam in there. Remove the lid and leave for another 2 minutes, then fluff with a fork. Stir through the shredded chicken, parsley and barberries or pomegranate seeds, if using, and leave for a couple of minutes to warm through.

DINNERTIME:
Serve.

TART: Once the rice is cooked, cover with a few layers of filo pastry, brushing with melted butter as you go, and bake at 180°C/350°F/Gas mark 4 for 10 minutes.

TWEAK: This is a great thing to do with leftover lamb shoulder (p.132) or neck (p.130). Instead of cooking the chicken thighs in the aromatic liquid, add the star anise and cinnamon to the onions and use chicken stock to cook the rice.

TOMORROW: Make burritos by warming some tortillas and spreading with guacamole (p.28), yogurt and chilli sauce. Add the plov and wrap. Leftover rice should be refrigerated within 4 hours and eaten within 2 days.

JAMBALAYA

SERVES 4–6

olive oil

300g/10½oz chorizo, ideally
    raw, cut into small chunks

6 boneless and skinless
    chicken thighs, quartered

salt and pepper

2 onions, peeled and
    finely chopped

2 sticks of celery,
    finely chopped

2 red peppers, deseeded
    and finely chopped

2 garlic cloves, peeled and
    thinly sliced

1 tsp cayenne pepper

1 tsp paprika

1 tbsp finely chopped
    fresh oregano

1 bay leaf

600ml/20fl oz/2½ cups chicken
    stock

300g/10½oz/generous
    1½ cups long-grain rice

It is only a small hop, skip and jump from the *plov* (p.138) to the jambalaya. Both dishes take the four principal constituents of vegetables, meat, stock and rice, and both are as comforting an affair as you could wish for. Yet in many ways, they are very different beasts. Jambalaya is a wetter, stickier business, and seems somehow more about the meat than the rice. It is, I like to imagine, what Grandpa Elliott was thinking about when he pulled the magnificent face below [photograph by Edu Hawkins].

Serve with a green salad and red pepper stew (p.174).

UP TO 6 HOURS AHEAD:

Heat a little oil in a large, heavy-bottomed saucepan over a medium heat and fry the chorizo until the meat is crisp and the oil is copper-coloured. Using a slotted spoon, remove the chorizo and set aside. Add the chicken to the pan and brown on both sides, seasoning with salt and pepper as you go. You'll need to do this in batches. Remove from the pan and reduce the heat.

Add the onions, celery, peppers and garlic, season with salt and pepper, and cover. Cook for 20 minutes until soft. Add the cayenne, paprika, oregano, bay leaf and stock, and bring to a boil. Return the meat to the pan and gently simmer for 30 minutes. Set aside or continue to the next step.

UP TO 1 HOUR AHEAD:

If necessary bring back to a simmer, then add the rice. Stir, cover and cook for 15 minutes, then take off the heat and leave for 5 minutes with the lid still on. Check for seasoning. If leaving for longer, keep warm in a very low oven (110°C/225°F/Gas mark ¼ or lower).

DINNERTIME:

Serve the jambalaya with Tabasco sauce.

TART: For a more Creole edge, add chopped tomatoes with the vegetables, and whole, cooked prawns at the end of cooking, leaving for a few minutes to warm through.

TWEAK: Instead of chorizo, try the more traditional *andouille*, a smoked sausage, which can be found in specialist shops or online.

TOMORROW: Turn into a soup by adding a good few ladlefuls of chicken stock and warming through. Eat with a crusty baguette. Leftover rice should be refrigerated within 4 hours and eaten within 2 days.

POACHED CHICKEN WITH PEAS, ONION AND BACON

SERVES 6

olive oil

200g/7oz pancetta or
    bacon, cubed

20 baby onions, covered in
    boiling water for a minute
    and then peeled

2 sticks of celery,
    finely chopped

salt and pepper

2 garlic cloves, peeled and
    finely chopped

a few sprigs of thyme

1 bay leaf

4–5 chicken wings

250ml/9fl oz/generous 1 cup
    dry white wine

6 supremes of chicken
    (breasts with the wing
    attached) or chicken
    breasts, skin on

500g/1lb 2oz shelled peas

For the mint and parsley oil

a small handful of mint leaves

25g/1oz parsley, leaves only

3 tbsp olive oil

juice of 1 lemon

TART: The broth could happily take a few wild mushrooms or, for even more of a one-pot dish, add new potatoes along with the chicken.

TWEAK: Try this with a whole chicken, leaving out the wings, covering and gently poaching for 1½ hours.

TOMORROW: Slice leftover chicken, then fry in garlic and spices and wrap in a warm flatbread with lots of salad leaves, yogurt and a punchy chilli sauce.

Chicken seems – finally – to be unshackling itself of the perception that it is a dull, homogenous protein. Welfare standards are improving, chickens are happier, and their meat has infinitely more flavour than it used to. When cooked with care and a few herbs or spices to help it along, it is the greatest all-rounder in the cook's arsenal. Don't ever feel like it's a cop-out to serve chicken.

UP TO A DAY AHEAD:

Heat a little oil in a large saucepan over a medium heat and fry the bacon until crisp and golden. Turn the heat down, add the onions and celery, season with salt and pepper, cover and cook over a low heat for 10 minutes. Add the garlic, thyme, bay, chicken wings and wine. Top up with water and bring to a boil. Skim off any scum and gently simmer for 2 hours, skimming when necessary. Discard the chicken wings, cool and chill.

UP TO 2 HOURS AHEAD:

To make the mint and parsley oil, finely chop the herbs and mix with the oil and lemon juice. Season with a pinch of salt, cover and set aside.

1 HOUR AHEAD:

Put the stock in a pan over a medium heat and bring to a gentle simmer.

Meanwhile, heat a little oil in a non-stick pan over a medium-high heat and add the chicken supremes, skin side down. Cook for 2–3 minutes on each side until golden, then add to the stock. Poach – just below a simmer – for 40–45 minutes.

Remove the chicken from the stock and rest in a warm place.

3–5 MINUTES AHEAD:

Add the peas to the stock and simmer for 3 minutes.

DINNERTIME:

Serve in large bowls or plates: tip in a generous ladleful of the peas, bacon, onion and stock. Sit the chicken on top and finish with a few flicks of mint and parsley oil.

POT-ROAST PARTRIDGE WITH QUINCE AND CHESTNUTS

SERVES 4

6 rashers of streaky bacon, chopped

1 tbsp olive oil

50g/1¾oz/4 tbsp butter

4 partridges, plucked, gutted and cleaned

salt and pepper

1 large quince, quartered and cored

1 onion, peeled and quartered

4 garlic cloves, peeled and squashed with the flat of a knife

150ml/5fl oz/⅔ cup Madeira or medium sherry

400ml/14fl oz/scant 1¾ cups chicken stock

200g/7oz cooked, peeled chestnuts, roughly chopped

a handful of woody herbs – thyme, rosemary, whatever you have to hand

The partridge is a beautiful bird, plump yet lean, and only mildly gamcy compared with, say, a grouse. They're in season from the beginning of September to the end of January, thus tying in rather neatly with when the fat, sharp quince is drooping from its bough.

As with much game, and particularly pheasant, partridge can become dry if you're not careful – pot-roasting is a good way of side-stepping this problem. This cooking method is also very easy-going: you can do the preparation hours in advance, then pop the whole thing in the oven and forget about it for 45 minutes.

Serve with creamed sprouts (p.168) or red cabbage (p.166).

UP TO 6 HOURS AHEAD:

Put a large ovenproof pan over a medium-high heat and add the bacon and a drop of oil. Fry until crisp, then remove from the pan, using a slotted spoon, and set aside. Add half the butter and brown the birds all over, seasoning with salt and pepper as you go. Remove from the pan. Add the remaining butter and brown the quince, then remove. Add the onion and fry until golden, then take off the heat and set aside. Cover and chill.

1 HOUR AHEAD:

Preheat the oven to 180°C/350°F/Gas mark 4. Take the partridges out of the fridge.

Put the pan with the onion over a medium heat. Add the garlic and Madeira or sherry and simmer for a minute, then return the partridge and the quince to the pan, along with the stock, chestnuts and herbs. Bring to a gentle boil, cover and put in the oven for 45 minutes. Remove from the oven and leave to rest.

DINNERTIME:

Serve each partridge with a wedge of quince and onion and a good spoonful of the cooking liquor, including plenty of chestnuts.

TART: For a richer sauce, strain the cooking juice into a pan and bring to a gentle boil. Enrich with 25g/1oz/2 tbsp butter that has had 2 tbsp of plain flour beaten into it, and serve over the birds.

TWEAK: Wrap each bird in a couple of rashers of bacon and brown until crisp, then cook as above.

TOMORROW: Use the cooking juices as a base for a rich, gamey risotto. Any leftover scraps of meat could find their way in, too.

ROAST SUPREME OF GUINEA FOWL
WITH SHERRY AND GRAPES

SERVES 6

2 tsp finely chopped
    thyme leaves
1 tsp finely chopped rosemary
1 garlic clove, peeled and
    crushed to a paste
100g/3½oz/7 tbsp butter,
    softened
salt and pepper
6 supremes of guinea fowl
olive oil
200ml/7fl oz/generous ¾ cup
    medium-dry sherry
100ml/3½fl oz/7 tbsp chicken
    stock
200g/7oz grapes, halved

Guinea fowl remains an inexplicably underused bird – it's got something of the pheasant about it (but without the propensity to dry out), it's no more expensive than a decent chicken, and it's lovely to cook with. So I say we should be cooking with it more.

Supremes are the breasts with the wing still attached. If you can't find any, then buy two whole guinea fowl and cleave in half down the middle, cooking for 15 minutes longer.

Serve with braised radicchio (p.177).

UP TO A DAY AHEAD:

Beat the thyme, rosemary and garlic into the butter and season with salt and pepper. Ease the skin of the birds away from the flesh and carefully spread the herb butter underneath the skin. Put in a roasting pan, cover and chill.

2 HOURS AHEAD:

Take the guinea fowl out of the fridge.

1 HOUR AHEAD:

Preheat the oven to 200°C/400°F/Gas mark 6.

Drizzle the guinea fowl with olive oil and roast for 30 minutes, or until the juices run clear when the thickest part is pierced with a thin sharp knife. Remove to a warm place to rest. Put the roasting pan over a high heat and add the sherry, scraping up all the sticky bits in the pan. Simmer for a couple of minutes, then add the stock and the grapes. Simmer for another 5 minutes and taste for seasoning.

DINNERTIME:

Serve the guinea fowl with the grapes and a good spoonful of gravy.

TART: Bit tarty already, this, though if you feel the urge to wrap the guinea fowl in Parma ham then follow that urge.
TWEAK: Roast whole grouse for 12 minutes at 220°C/425°F/Gas mark 7 and then follow the same recipe for making the grape gravy.
TOMORROW: Thinly slice leftover guinea fowl and toss through a green salad with a handful of croutons.

SPICED QUAIL WITH HERBY COUSCOUS AND YOGURT

SERVES 6

12–18 quails

4 tbsp olive oil

1 tbsp ground coriander

1 tsp ground cumin

1 tsp hot smoked paprika

a pinch of ground cloves

2 garlic cloves, peeled and
crushed to a paste

2 tbsp honey

juice of 1 lemon

For the couscous

2 large onions, peeled and
finely chopped

2 garlic cloves, peeled and
finely chopped

100g/3½oz/generous ½ cup
sultanas (golden raisins)

salt and pepper

1 litre/1¾ pints/4 cups chicken
or vegetable stock

500g/1lb 2oz/scant 3 cups
couscous

a good handful of herbs –
parsley, coriander
and chives

zest and juice of 1 lemon

To serve

lemon wedges

200g/7oz/generous ¾ cup
Greek-style yogurt

This is a variation of a dish that Lucas Hollweg made when he cooked at the Secret Larder. It was a gorgeous, sticky, hands-on operation – one for the kitchen roll, as opposed to the best napkins. Introduce the birds to their marinade the day before you need them; on the day, all you need do is get the quails out of the fridge and into the oven. Quails are quite forgiving birds, so don't be afraid to give them another 5 minutes to crisp up if that's what they need. They're small creatures, so you need at least two each, though a very hungry person could probably demolish three.

Serve with honey-roasted carrots (p.156) or a simple green salad.

UP TO A DAY AHEAD:

Find a big bowl or two for the quails. Heat the oil in a frying pan over a medium heat, then add the spices and cook for a minute or so, stirring continuously. Add the garlic and cook for another 30 seconds, then remove from the heat and tip into a mixing bowl. Add the honey and lemon juice, along with a good pinch of salt. Leave until completely cool, then rub all over the birds. Cover and chill.

As the base for the couscous, heat a good slug of oil in a large saucepan over a medium-low heat and add the onions. Cook for about 30 minutes, stirring regularly, until sweet and sticky. Add the garlic and sultanas and season with salt and pepper. Cook for a further minute, then take off the heat.

2 HOURS AHEAD:

Take the birds out of the fridge.

1 HOUR AHEAD:

Preheat the oven to 220°C/425°F/Gas mark 7. Put the birds in a large roasting pan, with a little space between them. Spoon over any extra marinade that might be lurking in the bottom of the mixing bowl.

30 MINUTES AHEAD:

Roast the quails for 20 minutes. Rest for 5 minutes.

Meanwhile, bring the stock to a boil. Stir the couscous through the onion mixture, then pour the stock over the couscous until just covering. Stir briefly, then cover with a tea towel and leave for 5 minutes. Roughly chop the herbs and stir through the couscous, along with the lemon juice and zest and a good pinch of salt.

DINNERTIME:
Serve the quails and couscous with a lemon wedge and a dollop of yogurt.

TART: Harissa would make an excellent accompaniment here. I'm a particular fan of Belazu's rose harissa.

TWEAK: Try this with poussins, allowing one per person and roasting for about 40 minutes.

TOMORROW: Couscous makes a good office lunch, while leftover quail would be delicious jointed and served in a salad of lettuce, herbs and red onion.

POT-AU-FEU

SERVES 8–10

1 small ox tongue, weighing
    1–1.5kg/2¼ –3¼lb
500g/1lb 2oz beef brisket,
    topside or silverside
300g/10½oz whole piece of
    pancetta or bacon
1 piece of veal marrow bone
    (optional)
1 bay leaf
a few sprigs of thyme
10 peppercorns
salt
6 large sausages, twisted in
    the middle and cut in half
500g/1lb 2oz slender carrots,
    peeled
4 onions, peeled and
    quartered through the root
12 garlic cloves, peeled
1 white cabbage, outer
    leaves removed, cut into
    wedges through the root
500g/1lb 2oz turnips or swede
    (rutabaga), peeled and
    chopped into chunks

To serve

a pot of Dijon mustard
a jar of cornichons
    (small gherkins)
crusty baguette or
    boiled potatoes

I first cooked *pot-au-feu* for my friend Ed's thirtieth birthday. He had requested it specifically, wet-lipped and wide-eyed, after seeing the great Raymond Blanc cooking it on the telly. It's quite an involved process but is, I assure you, worth the effort – an incredibly humble preparation that is also somehow magnificently grandiose. It is a dish for a special occasion. You will need the biggest saucepan in the house.

UP TO A DAY AHEAD:

Put the tongue in a very large saucepan and cover with water. Bring to a boil, simmer for a few minutes, then drain and rinse the tongue and the pan. Return the tongue to the pan along with the brisket, pancetta, marrow bone (if using), bay leaf, thyme and peppercorns and cover with water, adding a generous pinch of salt. Slowly bring to a boil, skimming off any scum. Cook just below a simmer for 3–4 hours, continuing to skim the surface. Take care not to let it boil, in order to maintain a clear broth.

Add the sausages and all the vegetables and cook for a further hour, then cool and chill, or continue.

UP TO 2 HOURS AHEAD:

Remove the tongue from the pan. Gently warm the broth and meat, if necessary. Meanwhile, peel the tongue, trim any gristle from the connective end, then slice. Arrange on a large serving plate or in a roasting pan. Slice the brisket and pancetta and arrange with the sausages alongside the sliced tongue. Discard the marrow bone if using. Garnish with the vegetables, if there's room, otherwise put them in a different dish and spoon plenty of the broth over both. Cover with foil and keep warm in a very low oven (110°C/225°F/Gas mark ¼ or lower) until ready to serve.

DINNERTIME:

Dish up the *pot-au-feu* on a large plate, or plate individually, and serve with mustard, cornichons and bread or potatoes.

TART: In terms of the meat you use, this is very tartable, especially if you're serving more people. Try adding some oxtail and/or short ribs.

TWEAK: The Italian *bollito misto* is a delicious cousin of this dish. Omit the vegetables and serve the boiled meats with salsa verde (p.128).

TOMORROW: The broth can be frozen and used for soups and stews, while the meat is going to make a hell of a sandwich.

RABBIT BLANQUETTE

SERVES 6–8

50g/1¾oz/4 tbsp butter

2 onions, peeled and
finely chopped

2 sticks of celery,
finely chopped

2 large carrots, peeled and
finely chopped

2 garlic cloves, peeled
and sliced

salt and pepper

2 rabbits, jointed

2 litres/3½ pints/2 quarts
chicken stock

1 bay leaf

300g/10½oz button
mushrooms, quartered

20 baby onions, covered in
boiling water for a few
minutes and then peeled

100ml/3½fl oz/7 tbsp dry
white wine

300ml/10fl oz/1¼ cups double
(heavy) cream

a squeeze of lemon juice

a small handful of parsley,
finely chopped

A blanquette – less to do with a blanket than with the dish's pale hue (despite the comfort it bestows) – is traditionally made using veal. But why not rabbit? It's delicious, lean and sustainable. If you can't find rabbit, however, then by all means use British rose veal, or even lamb.

Serve with roasted root vegetables (p.160) or potatoes with bacon and onion (p.154).

UP TO 2 DAYS AHEAD:

Melt half the butter in a large saucepan over a low heat. Add the onions, celery, carrots and garlic, season with salt and pepper, and cover. Cook for 20 minutes, until softened, stirring occasionally.

Add the rabbit, stock and bay leaf and bring to a boil. Skim off any scum if necessary, then simmer gently for 1½ hours.

Meanwhile, melt the remaining butter in another pan and add the mushrooms and onions. Season with salt and pepper and cook for a couple of minutes without colouring, then add the wine. Simmer for a minute, cover and cook for a further 10 minutes.

Transfer the rabbit to this pan, cool and chill. Reserve the cooking liquor.

30 MINUTES AHEAD:

Warm the rabbit over a medium heat, if necessary, then add a couple of spoonfuls of the cooking liquor and the cream and swirl to combine. Gently simmer for 10 minutes, and keep warm until ready to serve.

DINNERTIME:

Serve the rabbit blanquette with a squeeze of lemon juice and a scattering of parsley, making sure that everyone gets a few baby onions and mushrooms.

TART: A tart and tweak combo would be an earthy mixture of mushrooms, such as chanterelles, chestnut (cremini) and oyster mushrooms.

TWEAK: Try with chunks of lamb shoulder instead of rabbit, or, for a quicker version, use chunks of lamb loin, which will only need about 15 minutes' cooking.

TOMORROW: This will improve with time, and leftovers freeze very well.

Vegetables and sides

The attitude towards side dishes is arguably what distinguishes an average home cook from a good one. Approached as an after-thought or an irritating necessity, then they'll do little but detract from the central component. But if taken as something that can really make the whole affair sing, they can elevate the main course from the everyday to a dish that is altogether more exciting.

Thankfully, it's not difficult. If your default mode is to boil a few carrots and peas and lob them onto the plate as a cursory nod towards getting your five-a-day, then consider for a second what you can do to enhance this. The first person to cook carrots with butter, white wine, thyme and sugar can't have spent days dreaming it up, and yet even something as straightforward as this both improves flavours immeasurably and demonstrates a willingness to make an extra but important effort.

A FEW THINGS TO KEEP IN MIND:

- Don't worry about smearing purées and quenelling mash – most, if not all, sides can just be plonked in the middle of the table for everyone to dig into. It's familiar, and generous, and much easier for you.
- If you're taking the do-ahead option, then greens can be blanched and refreshed in advance. This simply means boiling until almost cooked, draining, and plunging into iced water. This prevents overcooking and keeps the colour. You can then reheat at the last minute.
- A sharp knife will be your best friend when prepping vegetables, as will a good vegetable peeler.

POTATO SALAD WITH ANCHOVY AND LOVAGE

SERVES 6–8
750g/1lb 10oz small
    new potatoes
salt and pepper
a handful of lovage leaves,
    roughly chopped
12 anchovy fillets,
    finely chopped
3 tbsp finely chopped shallot
1 tbsp Dijon mustard
juice of 1 lemon
olive oil

This is a potato salad with big flavours. Lovage is how celery would taste if it drank less water. (If you can't find/don't fancy lovage, use parsley.) Anchovy is, well, it's anchovy. I say embrace the nostril-clearing brawn of these spuds.

Serve warm or cold with a fish dish or something picnicky.

UP TO A DAY AHEAD:

Put the potatoes in a pan of salted water and bring to a boil. Simmer for 20 minutes or so, until cooked through, then drain.

Toss with the lovage, anchovy, shallot, mustard and lemon juice. Add a few slugs of olive oil and season with pepper. Serve while hot, or cover and chill until dinnertime.

DINNERTIME:

Serve. If you have chilled the salad and prefer to serve warm, warm the potatoes through either in the oven at its lowest setting for 15 minutes, or in a microwave.

TART: For a richer experience, mix a few dollops of crème fraîche through with the other ingredients.
TOMORROW: The salad will keep for a few days in the fridge.

DAUPHINOIS POTATOES

SERVES 6–8

1kg/2¼lb floury potatoes,
    such as Maris Piper or
    King Edward
500ml/18fl oz/generous 2 cups
    double (heavy) cream
2 garlic cloves, peeled
    and squashed with
    the flat of a knife
a sprig of thyme
1 bay leaf
25g/1oz/2 tbsp butter
nutmeg
salt and pepper
50g/1¾oz Gruyère cheese,
    grated

In the depths of chilly winter, there are few vegetable dishes more **deliciously, decadently comforting than dauphinois potatoes, aka *gratin dauphinois*. Layers of soft spud, garlicky cream and a crust on top that could be part of a drum kit, all make this a potato dish of kings. Almost literally – in France, the expression *le gratin* is slang for 'the upper crust'.**

This is a fantastic do-ahead dish to have up your sleeve – or indeed in your fridge – and will transform a simple baked ham or lamb chop supper into a real treat.

UP TO A DAY AHEAD:

Slice the potatoes – peel first, if you wish, though I rarely bother – and put in a pan of salted water. Bring to a boil and simmer for 7 minutes, then drain.

Meanwhile, put the cream, garlic and herbs in a pan over a medium heat and bring to a boil. Take off the heat immediately and leave to infuse for 20 minutes or so. Preheat the oven to 200°C/400°F/Gas mark 6.

Rub an ovenproof dish with a little of the butter, and add a layer of potatoes. Season with a grating of nutmeg, salt and pepper and pour over a splash of the cream. Continue layering thus until you've used up your spuds, then tip over the rest of the cream, discarding the garlic and herbs. Dot the top with the remaining butter and scatter over the cheese. Bake for 45 minutes.

Serve, or cool, cover and chill.

1 HOUR AHEAD:

If the potatoes have been chilled, preheat the oven to 120°C/250°F/Gas mark ½ and warm through for 30 minutes or so. If you're using the oven for something else and it's hotter then that's fine, though the potatoes will reheat quicker. Serve when ready.

TART: This works beautifully as a main in its own right, with pieces of ham or smoked mackerel interspersed throughout. Serve with a green salad.

TWEAK: For boulangère potatoes – a less rich version – use chicken or vegetable stock instead of cream, and sliced onions between each layer; this may need another 10–15 minutes in the oven.

TOMORROW: Leftovers freeze, if you have masses, or otherwise can be reheated for a good lunch with some ham and mustard.

POTATOES WITH BACON AND ONION

SERVES 4–6

olive oil

10 rashers of smoked streaky
    bacon, chopped

2 large onions, peeled and
    very roughly chopped

salt and pepper

2 garlic cloves, peeled and
    finely sliced

4 large potatoes, quartered –
    your choice, but I like
    red-skinned Désirée for this

2 litres/3½ pints/2 quarts
    chicken stock

a bunch of parsley,
    roughly chopped

When I wrote my first book, Dad was particularly miffed that this – his – potato recipe had been omitted. The fact that there were no other potato dishes in the book wasn't a good enough excuse – the recipe ought to be recorded for posterity. So here it is. It's very much a dad sort of dish, a chuck it in the pan and read the paper kind of preparation, which on a Sunday morning – or indeed Wednesday afternoon – suits me fine. An all-rounder, this, but try it with roast chicken or venison.

UP TO A DAY AHEAD:

Heat a little oil in a large saucepan and cook the bacon until crisp. Add the onions, season with salt and pepper and continue to cook, stirring occasionally, until the onions have taken on a bit of colour. Add the garlic, potatoes and chicken stock. Bring to a boil and simmer for 25–30 minutes, until the potatoes are cooked. Serve, or cool, cover and chill.

45 MINUTES AHEAD:

Put the potatoes over a medium heat and warm up. Leave ticking over on a low heat until ready to serve.

DINNERTIME:

Serve the potatoes, with bacon, onion, a spoonful of stock and a scattering of parsley.

TART: Add finely chopped sage at the end along with the parsley.
TWEAK: Fry the bacon and set aside before boiling the potatoes. Scatter crisp bacon over at the end. If feeding vegetarians, leave out the bacon and use vegetable stock.
TOMORROW: Slice leftover spuds and use for a Spanish omelette.

HONEY-ROASTED CARROTS
WITH ZA'ATAR

SERVES 6–8

1 tbsp pine nuts
1kg/2¼lb carrots, peeled
    and thickly sliced
3 tbsp olive oil
2 tbsp runny honey
2 tbsp za'atar
salt and pepper

There is a certain amount of wiggle room necessary when writing a recipe for carrots, caused principally by the inevitability of the cook (and/or one of their immediate family) munching about 20 percent of the things raw while peeling and chopping. This is no bad thing. Carrots are not chips, and will do you good, even if they won't make you see in the dark.

Za'atar is a herb mix and you can find it in most supermarkets. It often contains salt, so taste the carrots before you go crazy with the seasoning.

UP TO A DAY AHEAD:

Preheat the oven to 220°C/425°F/Gas mark 7.

In a dry frying pan, toast the pine nuts over a medium heat, taking care not to burn them. Set aside.

Toss the carrots with the oil, honey and za'atar, and season with salt and pepper to taste. Roast for 40 minutes, shaking the pan every once in a while. Serve, or cool, cover and chill.

30 MINUTES AHEAD:

Gently warm the carrots through in a low oven.

DINNERTIME:

Scatter the toasted pine nuts over the carrots and serve.

TART: Depending on what you're serving this with, a mixture of herbs would work nicely, tossed through at the last minute – mint, parsley and coriander are favourites, but tarragon also works well.
TWEAK: Instead of using za'atar, use a couple of spoonfuls of dukkah (p.30).
TOMORROW: Make a soup by softening an onion and a little garlic, then adding a chopped potato and stock. Simmer with the leftover carrots until the potato is cooked, then blend until smooth.

BAKED ONIONS WITH ANCHOVY AND CREAM

SERVES 6

3 large onions
6–9 anchovy fillets
300ml/10fl oz/1¼ cups double (heavy) cream
25g/1oz/¼ cup fine dried breadcrumbs
1 tsp chopped thyme
salt and pepper
olive oil

It's all too rare that an onion gets to play a lead role in a dish. More often than not, the poor fella finds himself hacked to pieces and cooked into submission before everyone else is piled on top of him. He is the Duncan in *Macbeth*, Mufasa in *The Lion King*. But not this time. Here the sweet little champion has a soliloquy all of his own, with just a little help from the cream, anchovy and breadcrumbs.

This dish is particularly good with roasted lamb or pork belly.

UP TO A DAY AHEAD:
Preheat the oven to 190°C/375°F/Gas mark 5.

Halve the onions through the root and then peel. Trim the root without cutting it off entirely, and leave the remains of the stalk intact. Lay in an ovenproof dish, cut side facing upwards. Flop 2–3 anchovy fillets over the top of each onion, then pour over the cream. Scatter with breadcrumbs and thyme, and finish with a little salt, plenty of pepper and a flick of oil. Bake for 1 hour, until easily pierced with a knife.

Serve, or cool, cover and chill.

30 MINUTES AHEAD:
Warm in a low oven for 20–30 minutes.

DINNERTIME:
Serve.

TART: Whip a little Dijon mustard through the cream before tipping over the onions. Grate over a liberal amount of Gruyère or Parmesan cheese before cooking.
TWEAK: For a healthier version, omit the cream, but be relatively generous with the oil.
TOMORROW: Should you have one or two leftover, use them as the base for an onion soup.

ROASTED ROOT VEGETABLES

SERVES 6

1.5kg/3lb 5oz root vegetables,
   some or all of: carrots,
   celeriac, turnips, beetroot,
   parsnips, swede (rutabaga)
2 red onions, peeled and
   roughly chopped
1 garlic bulb, cloves
   separated but not peeled
a small handful of rosemary
a small handful of thyme
salt and pepper
olive oil

If you're lucky enough to have a garden or allotment, then this is a nifty way of using up a surfeit of root vegetables. If you're not so lucky, then it's worth scooping up an armful of whatever you fancy from the greengrocer, or climbing into your neighbour's garden and digging away until they set the dog on you. It's wholesome and wintry and dead, dead easy, and will improve any Sunday roast.

UP TO 6 HOURS AHEAD:
Wash and trim (and peel if you prefer) the vegetables, and chop into vaguely even-sized dice of about 5cm/2in. Tip into a roasting pan with the onions, garlic and herbs. Season with plenty of salt and pepper and douse liberally with oil. Toss thoroughly. Cover.

1½ HOURS AHEAD:
Preheat oven to 200°C/400°F/Gas mark 6. Roast the vegetables for 1 hour, giving them a shake after 30 minutes. Keep warm until dinnertime.

DINNERTIME:
Serve.

TART: To make this into a vegetarian main dish, finish with chunks of feta cheese and toss through couscous with a big handful of chopped herbs.
TWEAK: In summer, I do a similar number but with new potatoes instead of the roots.
TOMORROW: The easiest soup you'll ever make: put leftover veg in a pan. Cover with stock and bring to a boil. Simmer for 5 minutes and blend.

CELERIAC AND HORSERADISH MASH

SERVES 4–6

1 medium celeriac,
    about 600g/1lb 5oz
1 large potato
salt and pepper
50g/1¾oz/4 tbsp butter
2 tbsp horseradish sauce

I love the nobbly, almost cerebral celeriac. For such an ugly brute it has a surprisingly mild, sweet flavour and is incredibly versatile – delicious when raw, as on p.43, happy sliced and baked with cream, or thoroughly mashed with plenty of butter and cracked pepper. It's a hardy, fibrous chap, so if you want a really smooth mash then chuck it in a blender. It won't go gluey like spuds.

This is a nigh-on unbeatable accompaniment to anything stewed and beefy or gamey.

UP TO A DAY AHEAD:

Wash the celeriac and trim off any straggly bits. Peel and cut into chunks, then put straight into a pan of cold water to prevent discoloration. Peel and chop the potato and add to the pan with a handful of salt. Bring to a boil and simmer for 25–30 minutes, until tender.

Drain and leave uncovered for a couple of minutes to steam off any excess moisture, then mash or blend with the butter and the horseradish. Season with a little salt and plenty of pepper to taste. Serve, or cool and chill.

30 MINUTES AHEAD:

Reheat over a low heat, stirring occasionally.

DINNERTIME:

Serve.

TART: To serve as a main course, stir some cooked smoked haddock through the mash and serve with a poached egg on top.
TWEAK: Swap the horseradish for mustard.
TOMORROW: Bubble and squeak: mix some chopped, cooked cabbage through the mash and fry in butter until crisp.

BRAISED SHALLOTS WITH CHILLI AND CHORIZO

SERVES 4–8

1 tbsp olive oil
125g/4½oz chorizo, ideally
    raw, chopped
4 banana or echalion shallots
    (the long ones)
1 long red chilli, deseeded
    and finely chopped
100ml/3½fl oz/7 tbsp medium-
    dry sherry
salt and pepper
a small handful of parsley,
    finely chopped

I could never claim to be an expert on Spanish food. The first time I went to Spain was during a brief and unsuccessful stint playing guitar in a folk band, when we spent a weekend in a van eating crisps and listening to bad radio, only to arrive at the venue, scarf a cold piece of pizza and try to get through our set before being tortilla'd off. Granted, the next two trips – a day in San Sebastián and a weekend in Barcelona – were more bountiful, but I'm no Claudia Roden. Consequently I'd be reluctant to suggest that anything was Spanish, *per se*, though with a dish like this, all the ducks seem to be in a row so, you know, *olé!*

UP TO A DAY AHEAD:

Heat the oil in a frying pan or sauté pan over a medium heat and add the chorizo. Fry until crisp. Meanwhile, halve and peel the shallots. Trim the root but don't cut it off, and leave the stalk if you like. Put them in the pan cut side down and cook for 3 minutes, until caramelized. Turn and cook for another 3 minutes. Add the chilli and sherry and simmer for 2 minutes. Season with salt and pepper, cover and cook over a low heat for 5 minutes. Serve with a scattering of parsley, or cover and chill.

20 MINUTES AHEAD:

Gently warm the shallots over a low heat. Scatter with chopped parsley before serving.

TART: This could be tarted quite literally – roll out puff pastry and lay the braised shallots and chorizo on top, along with a slice of Manchego cheese. Bake at 180°C/350°F/Gas mark 4 for 20 minutes.

TWEAK: A more British version: no chilli, bacon instead of chorizo, cider instead of sherry.

TOMORROW: Make the tart, as above, or use as the base of a punchy soup.

MIDDLE EASTERN(ISH) BEETROOT SALAD

SERVES 4–6

500g/1lb 2oz beetroot
salt and pepper
2 tsp coriander seeds
1 tsp cumin seeds
1 tsp caraway seeds
1 tsp sesame seeds
3 tbsp plain yogurt
juice of ½ lemon
3 tbsp olive oil
2 tbsp shelled pistachios,
    roughly chopped
a small handful of parsley,
    finely chopped

Is there a finer vegetable than the beetroot? In the depths of night, when considering this question, I will often concede that the onion just about clinches it – I could cook without beetroot for the rest of my life, sad as it would be; I couldn't cook without onions. Nonetheless, this is an unfair contest and, assuming the onion has a sick note from matron, the beetroot, in my mind, always romps home. It does well in most contexts – roasted or pickled, savoury or sweet (if you haven't tried beetroot brownies, then do) – and particularly with spices, as here.

This is a good picnic vegetable dish, or try serving it with a gently spiced fillet of salmon.

UP TO 2 DAYS AHEAD:

Put the beetroot in a pan of salted water and bring to a boil. Gently simmer until easily pierced with a skewer – 30–45 minutes, depending on the size of the beetroot. Drain and cool.

Meanwhile, toast the coriander, cumin, caraway and sesame seeds in a dry frying pan over a medium heat for 1 minute, shaking occasionally. Lightly crush in a pestle and mortar.

Peel the beetroot by hand – a rub of the thumb should take the skin away (the beetroot's, not yours, unless it's still too hot) – and slice, before tossing with the spices. Cover and chill.

Beat together the yogurt, lemon juice and olive oil, season with salt and pepper to taste, cover and chill.

1 HOUR AHEAD:

Take the beetroot out of the fridge – it's best served at room temperature.

DINNERTIME:

Arrange the beetroot on a serving plate and finish with the yogurt dressing and a scattering of pistachios and chopped parsley.

TART: There's already quite a lot going on here so I wouldn't.
TWEAK: Goatiness and beetroot go very well together, so swap the plain yogurt for goat's milk yogurt.
TOMORROW: This will keep for a couple of days and, with some bulgur wheat and a few greens, would make a grand desk lunch.

GLAZED TURNIPS

SERVES 4–6
500g/1lb 2oz small turnips
25g/1oz/2 tbsp butter
400ml/14fl oz/scant 1¾ cups
    chicken or vegetable stock
a sprig of thyme
salt and pepper

I briefly considered starting a campaign to celebrate the turnip. I don't understand how such a great ingredient could be so undervalued. Its peppery sweetness and affinity with beef should make it a regular winter vegetable, and yet it's something eaten even more seldom than a sprout, and with even less willing. So, why not – let's make the turnip popular again.

These go delightfully alongside wintry food – stews, pies, roasts, that kind of thing. I once made a turnip and blackberry pie after it was suggested to me by a reader... not such a good idea.

UP TO A DAY AHEAD:
Peel and quarter the turnips. Melt the butter in a sauté pan or saucepan and add the turnips, stock and thyme. Season with salt and pepper, then bring to a boil and simmer for 20–25 minutes over a medium heat, swishing and swirling the pan regularly, until the turnips can easily be pierced with a knife and the stock is reduced and sticky. Serve, or cool and chill.

15 MINUTES AHEAD:
Gently warm the turnips over a medium-low heat, stirring occasionally.

DINNERTIME:
Season with a pinch of salt and plenty of pepper, and serve.

TART: Fry a chopped onion and a little sliced garlic in the butter before adding the turnips, then continue as above, and finish with chopped sage.

TWEAK: In the interests of championing the turnip, I'm reluctant to suggest an alternative vegetable, though this does work well with swede, should you not be able to find any turnips.

TOMORROW: I like the sound of glazed turnips, sausages and eggs for breakfast...

CIDER-BRAISED RED CABBAGE

SERVES 6–8

25g/1oz/2 tbsp butter

1 large onion, peeled and finely sliced

salt and pepper

1 red cabbage, about 800g/1lb 12oz

1 cinnamon stick

2 star anise

2 cloves

a good grating of nutmeg

½ bottle (375ml/13fl oz/ 1½ cups) cider

125ml/4fl oz/½ cup cider vinegar

125g/4½oz/generous ½ cup dark brown sugar

a good handful of raisins

While many of the veg dishes can – as opposed to should – be done in advance, I would urge you to do this a day or two ahead if at all possible. Rather like a stew, the flavour only improves when the various elements of the dish have had some time to co-exist and cohere. Then it will be just the thing to enliven a game or roast pork dish.

UP TO 3 DAYS AHEAD:

Melt the butter in a large, heavy-bottomed pan over a low heat and add the onion. Season with salt and pepper and cook for 15 minutes.

Meanwhile, discard any grotty leaves from the cabbage, then quarter it and take out the core. Slice as finely as possible and add to the pan along with the remaining ingredients and plenty of salt and pepper. Stir over a medium heat until the sugar has dissolved. Bring to a boil, cover and simmer over a low heat for 2–3 hours, stirring occasionally. Take off the heat, cool and chill.

1 HOUR AHEAD:

Taste the cabbage for seasoning and pop back over a low heat to warm through. It should be sweet and sour and gently spiced.

DINNERTIME:

Serve.

TART: Add slices of apple towards the end of cooking. Crushed fennel seeds will go very well, too, particularly if serving with pork.

TWEAK: Instead of cider, try using 300ml/10fl oz/1¼ cups port.

TOMORROW: This will keep for a few days in the fridge. It's also delicious in a ham sandwich with plenty of mustard.

SPRING GREENS WITH GARLIC, LEMON AND ANCHOVY

SERVES 4–6

salt and pepper
500g/1lb 2oz spring greens
olive oil
2 garlic cloves, peeled
    and finely sliced
10 anchovy fillets,
    finely chopped
juice of ½ lemon

The temptation with spring greens, as indeed with a lot of green vegetables, is to pummel them with butter. There's something about fresh, green, healthy food that makes me want to compensate by adding a great big dollop of sweet, golden fat. It is of course not necessary, with a lick of olive oil and a squeeze of lemon being, if anything, more appropriate.

UP TO 6 HOURS AHEAD:

Get a bowl of iced water ready and bring a pan of salted water to a boil. Strip the leaves of the greens off their stalks. Finely chop the stalks and set aside, then roughly chop the leaves and drop them into the boiling water. Boil for 1 minute, then drain and plunge into the cold water. Leave for 5 minutes, drain and squeeze out any excess water. Cover and chill until needed.

5–10 MINUTES AHEAD:

Heat a little oil in a large frying pan, saucepan or wok, and add the garlic and chopped stalks. Fry for a minute or so, taking care not to burn the garlic, then add the anchovies and greens. Season with salt and pepper, and cook over a medium-high heat, stirring almost continuously, for 3–4 minutes. Add the lemon juice and stir again. Serve immediately.

TART: I often throw in a handful of chopped red chilli, or add some blanched peas and broccoli to the mix.
TWEAK: Try this with curly kale or cavolo nero.
TOMORROW: Finely chop leftovers and toss through pasta with a good grating of Parmesan, or add to a risotto.

CREAMED SPROUTS WITH BACON, MARSALA AND ALMONDS

SERVES 4–6

500g/1lb 2oz Brussels sprouts, outer leaves removed, halved through the root

salt and pepper

125g/4½oz smoked, streaky bacon, chopped

olive oil

100ml/3½fl oz/7 tbsp Marsala wine

50g/1¾oz/½ cup flaked (slivered) almonds

3 tbsp double (heavy) cream

There's always a bit of a tussle over the sprouts round ours come Christmas time. Grandpa's teeth aren't what they once were, which is to say in his mouth, and so he likes his sprouts cooked, what Mrs Beeton may have (but probably never) called, 'to buggery'. Everyone else, on the other hand, likes a bit of bite. We've tried various tacks – sprout purée with a little nutmeg was quite successful – but there's always room for variety, and so here's a new idea, which I plan to unleash on the Ramsden Christmas this year. That said, sprouts aren't just for Christmas...

UP TO A DAY AHEAD:

Fill a bowl with cold, iced water. Bring a pan of salted water to a boil and add the sprouts. Bring back to a boil and simmer for 2–3 minutes, drain, then plunge the sprouts directly into the cold water and leave for 5 minutes. Drain and shake dry, then cover and chill.

Put a non-stick frying pan or sauté pan over a medium heat and fry the bacon in a little oil until crisp. Add the Marsala and reduce by half, then take off the heat and leave to cool. Refrigerate if leaving overnight.

In a dry pan over a medium heat, toast the almonds for a minute or two, stirring regularly, until golden. Set aside in a bowl.

10 MINUTES AHEAD:

Put the pan with bacon in it over a medium heat. When it starts to fizzle, add the sprouts and the cream and bring back to a gentle boil. Season with salt and pepper and simmer for 3 minutes.

DINNERTIME:

Scatter the toasted almonds over the sprouts and serve.

TART: Fry a chopped onion along with the bacon until softened and lightly caramelized.

TWEAK: If you can't find Marsala, try Madeira, or a medium sherry instead.

TOMORROW: I'm quite partial to leftover sprouts as part of a fridge buffet – a term coined and defined by a publican friend Oisin Rogers as 'a solitary pursuit, best practised in silence, very late at night.' Roughly chopped, passed through mashed potato, swede or celeriac and then fried, makes a good bubble and squeak too.

BOSTON BAKED BEANS

SERVES 6–8

500g/1lb 2oz dried cannellini
    beans, soaked overnight,
    or 4 x 400g/14oz cans
2 red onions, peeled and
    finely chopped
2 garlic cloves, peeled and
    finely chopped
250g/9oz pancetta or bacon,
    chopped into big chunks
150g/5½oz/¾ cup molasses
    or dark brown sugar
    or 150ml/5fl oz/⅔ cup
    maple syrup
1 tbsp tomato purée
    (tomato paste)
4 tbsp English mustard
1 tbsp hot smoked paprika
1 cinnamon stick
2 cloves
1 bay leaf
salt and pepper

This dish benefits enormously from being cooked a day or two in advance and reheated. Great with any pork dish, from sausages to barbecued shoulder.

UP TO 2 DAYS AHEAD:
Preheat the oven to 150°C/300°F/Gas mark 2.

    If using soaked dried beans, rinse under a running tap then put them in an ovenproof pan. Add cold water to just cover the beans, bring to a boil and simmer until tender – 45 minutes to 1 hour. If using canned beans, drain and rinse, then simmer in a pan of water for 4–5 minutes.

    Take off the heat and add all the remaining ingredients along with a good twist of pepper, but no salt at this point. Give it a stir, cover and bake in the oven for 2–3 hours. Uncover and bake for a further hour. Serve, or cool and refrigerate.

30 MINUTES AHEAD:
Reheat over a low heat, stirring occasionally, until piping hot.

DINNERTIME:
Check for seasoning and add salt if necessary. Serve.

TART: An extra chilli kick would work nicely, so add some chopped fresh jalapeño. For a more decadent all-in-one dish, add a good grating of Cheddar cheese for the final hour's baking.
TWEAK: You can use pretty much any beans you like. Omit the pancetta for a vegetarian version.
TOMORROW: Beans on toast aside, you could add some chicken stock to the leftovers and simmer with chopped kale for a warming winter soup.

FLAGEOLET BEAN SALAD

SERVES 4–6

juice of ½ lemon

2 shallots, finely chopped

2 x 400g/14oz cans flageolet beans, drained and rinsed

1 small garlic clove, peeled and crushed to a paste

2 tomatoes, finely diced (deseeded and peeled if you prefer)

a good slug of olive oil

salt and pepper

a generous handful of leafy herbs – parsley, coriander, mint, basil

This is a handy storecupboard back-up for when you have a couple of cans of beans that need a home and some lamb chops that need a neighbour.

UP TO A DAY AHEAD:

Squeeze the lemon juice over the chopped shallots and set aside.

Cover the beans with water and bring to a boil. Simmer for 3–4 minutes. Drain and toss with the shallots, garlic, tomatoes and olive oil. Season with plenty of salt and pepper. Cover and chill, or proceed to the next step.

DINNERTIME:

Roughly chop the herbs and mix through the beans. Taste for seasoning and serve.

TART: If serving with lamb, or beef or chicken for that matter, I'd add some chopped anchovy, or try adding some toasted pine nuts for extra crunch.

TWEAK: The herbs you choose are entirely tweakable, though avoid woody herbs like thyme and rosemary.

TOMORROW: The salad will keep for a few days in the fridge and makes a good desk lunch.

LENTILS WITH FETA, ROCKET, CHILLI AND CROUTONS

SERVES 6–8

500g/1lb 2oz/generous
   2½ cups green lentils
150g/5½oz feta cheese,
   crumbled
2 red chillies, deseeded
   and finely chopped
50g/1¾oz rocket (arugula)
juice of 1 lemon
salt and pepper
2 tbsp olive oil
a few pieces of stale white
   bread, chopped
   into chunks

This is a summery preparation, best served at room temperature. Warm lentils will make the feta run and the rocket wilt, if you're not careful, so if you are serving this warm, make sure you do so pronto.

UP TO A DAY AHEAD:
Boil the lentils according to pack directions. Drain and leave to cool. Toss through the feta, chillies, rocket and lemon juice and season with salt and pepper. Cover and chill.

1 HOUR AHEAD:
Take the lentils out of the fridge to come up to room temperature.

15 MINUTES AHEAD:
Heat the oil over a medium heat in a frying pan and toss in the pieces of bread. Fry, turning occasionally, until crisp and golden. Season with a pinch of salt.

DINNERTIME:
Fold the croutons through the lentils and serve.

TART: To make this more of a one-pot supper, add some fried chorizo and finish with a poached egg.

TWEAK: For a gently spiced, Indian angle, swap the rocket for fresh coriander, and add 1 teaspoon garam masala with the chillies; replace the feta with chopped paneer. Instead of the bread, use bits of toasted naan.

TOMORROW: Store in the fridge and eat within a couple of days.

RED PEPPER STEW WITH 'NDUJA

SERVES 4–6
olive oil
1 onion, peeled and
    finely chopped
salt and pepper
1 garlic clove, peeled
    and thinly sliced
150g/5½oz 'nduja,
    deskinned if necessary
800g/1lb 12oz peppers –
    red, orange and yellow –
    deseeded and sliced
400g/14oz canned chopped
    tomatoes
a sprig of thyme
1 tsp sugar
a handful of basil leaves

'Nduja is an amazing soft and spicy sausage from Calabria in southern Italy. It's so soft, in fact, that you can spread it on toast, and so spicy that it ought to be used with caution. Buy it from Italian delis or online, either whole or in a jar.

This is quite a substantial side dish, and so is best served with something light such as poached chicken or grilled fish.

UP TO 2 DAYS AHEAD:
Heat a little oil in a sauté pan or frying pan over a low heat and add the onion. Season with salt and pepper and cook, stirring occasionally, for 15 minutes, until softened. Add the garlic and 'nduja and push around the pan, breaking up the sausage as you go. Once it's taken on some colour, add the peppers, tomatoes, thyme and sugar. Bring to a gentle boil, cover and simmer over a low heat for 40 minutes.

Uncover and cook for a further 20 minutes until reduced. Tear the basil leaves, stir through and serve, or cool, cover and chill.

30 MINUTES AHEAD:
Put the stew over a low heat and stir occasionally until warm.

DINNERTIME:
Taste for seasoning and adjust if necessary. Tear the basil leaves and stir through. Serve.

TWEAK: If you can't find 'nduja, use cooking chorizo instead, or omit altogether for a vegetarian dish.
TOMORROW: Briefly blend leftovers and use as a pasta sauce.

BUTTERED SAMPHIRE WITH GARLIC

SERVES 4

250g/9oz marsh samphire, any woody stalks discarded
40g/1½oz/3 tbsp butter
1 garlic clove, peeled and very finely chopped
salt and pepper
juice of ½ lemon

Amazing stuff, samphire. It has a crunch that is irresistible and a saltiness that, as one supper club guest noted floridly, reminds you that it has been washed twice daily by the tide. At least, marsh samphire will taste like that and marsh samphire is what you're most likely to find. Its cousin, rock samphire, is harder to track down, and more expensive to boot. So how do you find the marsh stuff? Well, it's in season in the spring through to early summer and there are two options: ask a fishmonger, who is bound to be able to get some for you, or head to the seaside with a plastic bag, a pair of scissors and a copy of Richard Mabey's *Food for Free* in your pocket.

Samphire's natural accompaniment is fish, though don't rule out serving it with something like grilled lamb.

UP TO 6 HOURS AHEAD:

Fill a bowl with cold water and a few ice cubes. Bring a big pan of water to a boil and chuck in the samphire. Boil for 30 seconds, drain, and plunge straight into the cold water. Leave for 10 minutes, drain again and shake dry. Cover and chill in the fridge, or continue to the next step.

5 MINUTES AHEAD:

Melt the butter in a sauté pan or large saucepan – or wok, even – over a medium heat. Add the garlic and cook for a minute or two, stirring continuously to avoid burning. Add the samphire and toss for a couple of minutes until warmed through. Taste for seasoning and only add salt if necessary, along with a good twist of pepper and a squeeze of lemon juice.

DINNERTIME:

Serve.

TART: As a course in its own right, serve the samphire on toast with a poached egg and/or hollandaise sauce.
TWEAK: Try pickling the samphire, using the method on p.85, replacing the cucumber with blanched samphire.
TOMORROW: Add to a lively fish stew, like the one on p.110, at the very last minute.

BRAISED RADICCHIO WITH HAZELNUTS AND SHERRY VINEGAR

SERVES 4–6

50g/1¾oz/scant ½ cup hazelnuts, roughly chopped

olive oil

1 onion, peeled and thinly sliced

salt and pepper

1 garlic clove, peeled and thinly sliced

1 tsp finely chopped rosemary

2 large heads of radicchio, halved and sliced

100ml/3½fl oz/7 tbsp sherry vinegar

It's the bitterness of radicchio – chicory's fat and blushing cousin – that appeals most, perfectly offsetting something rich and fatty like pork belly, as it's served at Polpo in London. Don't be too worried about overcooking – it can withstand a fair bit without going to mush, and you're not looking for full-on crunch here.

UP TO 6 HOURS AHEAD:

In a dry frying pan over a medium heat, lightly toast the hazelnuts until fragrant, taking care not to burn them. Set aside.

Heat a little oil in a large saucepan over a low heat and add the onion. Season with salt and pepper and cook for 15 minutes, stirring occasionally. Add the garlic and rosemary and cook for a further minute. Set aside or continue to the next step.

20 MINUTES AHEAD:

Put the pan over a medium heat and add the radicchio and sherry vinegar. Bring to a boil, cover and turn the heat to low. Cook for about 15 minutes, stirring occasionally, until completely wilted. Taste for seasoning.

DINNERTIME:

Scatter the toasted hazelnuts over the radicchio and serve.

TART: A generous grating of Parmesan cheese would seem like a good thing to do here. Crumbling over a little ricotta wouldn't be a bad idea either.

TWEAK: If you can't find radicchio, use chicory instead.

TOMORROW: Chop up any leftovers and fold through a risotto along with a couple of spoonfuls of ricotta.

COURGETTE GRATIN

SERVES 4–6

400ml/14fl oz/scant 1¾ cups
   double (heavy) cream
1 garlic clove, peeled and
   squashed with the
   flat of a knife
a good grating of nutmeg
salt and pepper
a knob of butter
600–800g/1lb 5oz–1lb 12oz
   courgettes (zucchini),
   sliced thinly on
   the diagonal
a good handful of grated
   Parmesan cheese
a handful of stale
   breadcrumbs

Come early autumn, the recipe for courgette bread on my website suddenly gets an extraordinary number of hits. This is down, no doubt, to all the gardeners wondering what on earth to do with their surfeit of courgettes. Possibilities are largely endless; this is a good start.

UP TO A DAY AHEAD:

Pour the cream into a saucepan, add the garlic and nutmeg, and season with salt and pepper. Gently bring to a boil then take off the heat. Leave to infuse for 10 minutes, then discard the garlic.

Meanwhile, preheat the oven to 180°C/350°F/Gas mark 4.

Rub an ovenproof dish with a knob of butter, then layer the courgettes in the dish, seasoning with salt and pepper as you go. Pour over the cream and top with the Parmesan and breadcrumbs. Bake for 40 minutes and serve, or leave to cool, cover and chill.

30 MINUTES AHEAD:

Warm through at about 190°C/375°F/Gas mark 5 – a little lower or higher if you have other things in the oven – for 10–15 minutes.

DINNERTIME:

Serve.

TART: A few chopped anchovies dotted among the courgettes work well.

TWEAK: For something richer and punchier, use slices of Taleggio cheese instead of Parmesan.

TOMORROW: Leftovers should be stored in the fridge and are best eaten within a couple of days.

BRAISED LETTUCE WITH PEAS AND HERBS

SERVES 4–6

salt and pepper

200g/7oz/1½ cups frozen peas

3 tbsp olive oil

2 shallots, peeled and
    finely chopped

a big handful of parsley,
    roughly chopped

2 Little Gem lettuce, leaves
    separated and washed

2 tsp tarragon leaves

a handful of mint leaves

juice of 1 lemon

a small handful of chervil
    leaves (optional)

The idea of cooking lettuce baffles some folk, I suppose understandably. If you've spent your life eating raw salads and enjoying the crunch and vitality of a lettuce leaf, then you might ask yourself why anyone would want to cook the stuff. I hope that once you've tried this, you will no longer ponder this question. It's sweet and moreish and every bit as lively as eating it raw, with the added bonus that it takes on so many more of the flavours around it. It's good with mackerel, either roasted and stuffed (p.112) or plain grilled. I'm very fond of it with a cottage pie, as well.

UP TO 6 HOURS AHEAD:

Bring a pan of salted water to a boil and add the peas. Cook for 2 minutes, then drain and run under a cold tap. Set aside.

Heat the oil in a large saucepan and fry the shallots until softened and golden. Set aside, or proceed to the next step.

15 MINUTES AHEAD:

Put the pan of fried shallots over a medium heat and add the parsley, lettuce and 100ml/3½fl oz/7 tbsp water. Season with salt and pepper, cover and cook over a medium-low heat for 7–10 minutes, until the lettuce has wilted.

Meanwhile, chop the tarragon and mint. Once the lettuce is cooked, stir the herbs through, with a squeeze of lemon juice and the peas.

DINNERTIME:

Serve the braised lettuce garnished with a few chervil leaves.

TART: Roughly chopped marinated artichoke hearts would work well, as would a few sliced radishes.

TWEAK: In the summer, try using broad beans instead of – or as well as – the peas.

TOMORROW: Blend leftovers as soon as possible with a little stock, then strain and chill for a summery soup.

Puddings

Pudding should always be a treat. Invite people round for dinner and they will expect a main course. They'll possibly hope for something to nibble on, or indeed dive into, beforehand. But to go to the extra effort of making a pudding is spoiling and generous and often unexpected.

It's also almost always do-aheadable. Unless you have a penchant for crêpes Suzette (I'd sympathize) or soufflé (and even then…) puddings tend to fall into the 'do and forget about' bracket. Pastries with brittle crusts and juicy fillings, cakes that need time to cool and set, ice creams, sorbets and jellies that will only work if you give them time, meringues with a hard shell and a chewy middle, all of these can be done so far ahead that you may forget you even bothered in the first place, seeing your guests off into the night only then to remember the pavlova sitting in the fridge.

I do love a bit of cheese, and it must be said that a decent piece of Cheddar or Stilton can be every bit as spoiling as the most sumptuous croquembouche, but every now and then the thing for which you most yearn is – and can only be – sweet.

Ice creams

My approach to ice cream – proper, custard-based ice cream – changed entirely when I interviewed Jim Fisher at his cookery school, Cook In France. Before that meeting, I'd generally avoided making the stuff, reluctant to stand over a bowl stirring custard until it thickened (and it never seemed to behave for me). Imagine my delight, then, when Jim explained that this was entirely unnecessary.

FOR A BASIC VANILLA ICE CREAM, put 600ml/20fl oz/2½ cups double (heavy) cream in a pan with a split vanilla pod and pop it over a medium-low heat. Slowly bring it to a boil. In a large, heavy bowl, with a tea towel folded underneath to stop the bowl from slipping, whisk 4–6 egg yolks (depending on size/how rich you like it) with about 100g/3½oz/½ cup caster (superfine) sugar until light and pale. When the cream is at a proper, rolling boil, dump it straight onto the egg yolks – no gentle pouring, straight on – whisking continuously as you do so. Don't stop whisking or you'll have scrambled eggs. Whisk for about another 30 seconds. Leave it for 2 minutes. Once the temperature has dropped to around 80°C/175°F, it'll be custard.

A caveat – Jim's method works best, I find, if you're using double cream. I tend to play the 'if you're going to eat ice cream you might as well do it properly' card, but if you'd like a lighter version using milk, or half and half, then you're best off employing the stand and stir method, which I'll explain in the recipe for honey and rosemary ice cream (p.184).

As for the ice-cream machine conundrum… They certainly help create a smoother ice cream, but as long as you're about the house, a vigorous whisk every few hours while the ice cream freezes does almost as good a job.

Unlike commercial ice cream, which contains preservatives and stabilizers, fresh ice cream is best eaten within a day or two of making.

HONEY AND ROSEMARY ICE CREAM

SERVES 6–8

600ml/20fl oz/2½ cups double (heavy) cream, or whole milk, or half and half

5 sprigs of rosemary

100g/3½oz/5 tbsp honey

4–6 egg yolks (depending on how rich you like it)

50g/1¾oz/¼ cup caster (superfine) sugar

Herbs in ice cream almost always work well, from Sarah Raven's basil ice cream (*Sarah Raven's Garden Cookbook*, Bloomsbury, 2007) – perfect with strawberries – to a thyme and ginger number I found in lord knows what book. It's a mellow, fragrant way to end a meal.

UP TO A DAY AHEAD (ALLOW 4 HOURS FOR FREEZING; 8 HOURS IF NOT USING AN ICE-CREAM MACHINE):

Put the cream, rosemary and honey in a pan and slowly bring to a boil. In a large heatproof bowl, whisk the egg yolks and sugar together until light and pale. When the cream is at a rolling boil, tip it directly onto the egg yolks, whisking furiously as you go. Whisk for about 30 seconds, until thick and smooth. Leave to cool for a couple of minutes.

If using milk, put the bowl over a pan of almost-simmering water and stir continuously until thickened. This can take 15–30 minutes. Avoid temptation to whack up the heat. It's ready when it coats the back of a spoon. Leave to cool.

Cover and chill overnight, or proceed to the next step. If you need to expedite the process, sit the bowl of custard in a bowl of iced water.

Strain the chilled custard and churn in an ice-cream machine. Alternatively, put in the freezer and whisk every couple of hours.

TART: Add 2 tablespoons of finely chopped crystallized ginger to the custard before churning.

TWEAK: Try with thyme instead of rosemary.

WHISKY ICE CREAM

SERVES 6–8

600ml/20fl oz/2½ cups double
  (heavy) cream
1 vanilla pod, split
4–6 egg yolks (depending on
  how rich you like it)
100g/3½oz/½ cup caster
  (superfine) sugar
100ml/3½fl oz/7 tbsp whisky

**We served this for Burns Night one year and it was a great success
– lightly smoked, sweet and earthy, just the thing after a big plate
of haggis. Which whisky you use is up to you: something peaty
from Islay is interesting but quite strong and, arguably, a waste
of good whisky, while a blend is more gentle and less complex.**

UP TO A DAY AHEAD (ALLOW 4 HOURS FOR FREEZING; 8 HOURS IF NOT USING AN ICE-CREAM MACHINE):

Put the cream and vanilla in a pan and slowly bring to a boil. In
a large heatproof bowl, whisk the egg yolks and sugar together
until light and pale. When the cream is boiling, tip it directly onto
the egg yolks, whisking continuously for about 30 seconds, until
thick and smooth. Cool, remove the vanilla pod and stir in the
whisky, then cover and chill, or proceed to the next step.

Strain the chilled custard and churn in an ice-cream
machine, or put in the freezer and whisk every couple of hours.

TART: Heat 100ml/3½fl oz/7 tbsp whisky until almost boiling, then
set on fire and pour over the ice cream. Serve immediately.
TWEAK: To give the ice cream an American accent, use bourbon
instead of whisky. Serve with the bread pudding on p.201.

RHUBARB CRUMBLE
ICE CREAM

SERVES 6–8

600ml/20fl oz/2½ cups double
    (heavy) cream
1 vanilla pod, split
4–6 egg yolks (depending on
    how rich you like it)
200g/7oz/1 cup caster
    (superfine) sugar
200g/7oz rhubarb
100ml/3½fl oz/7 tbsp water
For the crumble
35g/1¼oz/2½ tbsp butter,
    cubed
50g/1¾oz/7 tbsp plain
    (all-purpose) flour
35g/1¼oz/2½ tbsp soft
    brown sugar
a pinch of salt

This is a sure-fire winner, even for those who claim not to like rhubarb. Sweet and sour, creamy and crunchy, it ticks lots of boxes.

UP TO A DAY AHEAD (ALLOW 4 HOURS FOR FREEZING; 8 HOURS IF NOT USING AN ICE-CREAM MACHINE):

Put the cream and vanilla in a pan and slowly bring to a boil. In a large heatproof bowl, whisk the egg yolks and half the caster sugar together until light and pale. When the cream is boiling, tip it directly onto the egg yolks, whisking continuously for about 30 seconds, until thick and smooth. Set aside to cool, then cover and chill.

Chop the rhubarb into smallish pieces and put in a pan with the remaining caster sugar and the water. Cover the pan and simmer over a medium heat for 7–10 minutes, until softened but not mushy. Remove with a slotted spoon, cover and chill.

To make the crumble, preheat the oven to 180°C/350°F/ Gas mark 4. Rub the butter into the flour until it looks like large breadcrumbs, then mix in the brown sugar and salt. Tip onto a baking sheet and bake for 15–20 minutes until crisp and browned. Set aside.

Strain the custard through a sieve, then fold in the rhubarb. Break up the crumble and mix through, then churn in an ice-cream machine, or put in the freezer and whisk every couple of hours.

TART: Instead of using water with the rhubarb, try ginger wine.
TWEAK: Use crumbled amaretti biscuits instead of the crumble.

HAZELNUT, FENNEL AND KAHLÚA ICE CREAM

SERVES 6–8

600ml/20fl oz/2½ cups double (heavy) cream
1 vanilla pod, split
4–6 egg yolks (depending on how rich you like it)
100g/3½oz/½ cup dark brown sugar
100ml/3½fl oz/6 tbsp Kahlúa coffee liqueur
100g/3½oz/scant 1 cup chopped hazelnuts
2 tsp fennel seeds, crushed
a good pinch of sea salt

Kahlúa, a rum-based coffee liqueur, is one of those drinks that sits, arms folded, at the back of the drinks cupboard. You have vague memories of having needed it for something (was it a white Russian?) about five years ago, but since then it's really only taken up space where gin might go. So here's a fine way of making the most of its sweet, coffee'd notes.

UP TO A DAY AHEAD (ALLOW 4 HOURS FOR FREEZING; 8 HOURS IF NOT USING AN ICE-CREAM MACHINE):

Put the cream and vanilla in a pan and slowly bring to a boil. In a large heatproof bowl, whisk the egg yolks and sugar together until light and pale. When the cream is boiling, tip it directly onto the egg yolks, whisking continuously. Keep whisking for another 30 seconds, then leave to cool. Stir through the Kahlúa, cover and chill.

In a dry frying pan, toast the hazelnuts until golden. Set aside.

Strain the custard, then fold through three-quarters of the hazelnuts and all the fennel seeds. Churn in an ice-cream machine, or put in the freezer and whisk every couple of hours.

DINNERTIME:

Serve the ice cream with a scattering of toasted hazelnuts and a good pinch of sea salt.

TWEAK: You could omit the grog altogether, or use a spiced rum instead.

Sorbets

Ice cream's slimmer cousin, the sorbet is often just what you need at the end of a rich meal. In fustian food terms, it's generally seen as a palate cleanser – something to be treated as a run-up to a 'proper' pudding. Consider it thus if you like, though if you've just mown your way through two courses and there's a truffle or two to go with your coffee, then a little bowl of sorbet for pudding is hardly parsimonious.

CUCUMBER SORBET

SERVES 4–6

1 large cucumber, weighing
   500–600g/1lb 2oz–1lb 5oz
150g/5½oz/¾ cup caster
   (superfine) sugar
juice of ½ lemon

We have an open kitchen at the supper club, or rather, our living room and kitchen are all one, and so when the dishes get frisbee'd out to guests, it's hard to resist cocking an ear to gauge reaction. On the whole, people are far more interested in each other than the food – which is the way it should be – but every now and then I catch a satisfied (I think) groan or, even better, the room falls silent. Cucumber sorbet seems to have this effect, I think probably because most people are expecting something challenging and Hestonian, when in fact this is just cooling and clean and floral.

Like ice cream, sorbet is best eaten within a couple of days.

UP TO A DAY AHEAD:

Peel the cucumber and cut it in half lengthways. Scoop out the seeds and discard. Put the flesh in a blender with the sugar and lemon juice. Blend until smooth. Churn in an ice-cream machine, or put in the freezer, whisking every couple of hours to prevent ice crystals forming, until frozen.

TART: Pour over a shot of chilled gin before serving.
TWEAK: Serve as an accompaniment to salmon tartare (p.85).

MANDARIN SORBET

SERVES 6–8
12 mandarins,
   6 of them zested
juice of 1 lemon
150g/5½oz/generous 1¼ cups
   icing (confectioners') sugar

If the cucumber sorbet (p.188) is a summery number, this couldn't be more of a Christmas dish, the mandarin's peak being December. Its cousins the clementine and the tangerine will for me always be associated with the festive period, but for cooking purposes I find the perfume of the mandarin slightly more interesting. Nevertheless, both those relatives will do a fine job in the absence of mandarins.

UP TO A DAY AHEAD:
Peel and blend, or thoroughly juice, all the mandarins, then pass through a sieve. Mix with the zest of 6 mandarins, the lemon juice and sugar. Taste and add a little more sugar if necessary – it loses sweetness when frozen, so if anything it should be a little over-sweet. Churn in an ice-cream machine, or put in the freezer, whisking every couple of hours to prevent ice crystals forming, until frozen.

TART: It's a bit kitsch but you could carefully remove the segments of 6–8 of the fruits in order to serve the sorbet in the mandarin shell.
TWEAK: As I say, tangerines or clementines will work well too.

MELON SORBET

SERVES 6–8
1 ripe cantaloupe or
   charentais melon
300g/10½oz/1½ cups caster
   (superfine) sugar
200ml/7fl oz/generous ¾ cup
   Champagne or Prosecco
juice of ½ lemon

A rather decadent sorbet, with a nip of Champagne to lift it.

UP TO A DAY AHEAD:
Quarter the melon, scoop out the seeds and discard, then cut away the flesh and blend with the sugar, Champagne or Prosecco and lemon juice. Churn in an ice-cream machine, or put in the freezer, whisking every couple of hours to prevent ice crystals forming, until frozen.

TART: I think Champagne is quite enough tarting for this sorbet.
TWEAK: Instead of a fizzy wine, try a sweet white muscat, using only 150g/5½oz/¾ cup sugar.
TOMORROW: Leave the sorbet in the fridge and serve as a chilled soup, either as a starter or pudding, the following evening.

ESPRESSO SORBET

SERVES 6–8

100g/3½oz/½ cup caster
　(superfine) sugar
2 tbsp strong ground coffee
300ml/10fl oz/1¼ cups water,
　1 minute off the boil
2 tbsp Kahlúa coffee liqueur

The trick here is ferociously strong coffee, tempered with a tot of sugar syrup and a glug of Kahlúa. Best not served in the evening to anyone of a sleepless disposition.

UP TO A DAY AHEAD:

Put the sugar in a pan with 100ml/3½fl oz/7 tbsp water and bring to a boil over a medium heat, stirring until the sugar has dissolved. Simmer for 3 minutes, then take off the heat.

Put the coffee in a bowl, add the just-boiled water and brew for 4 minutes, then strain. If you have a cafetière, make the coffee that way. It's important that the water has had a minute off the boil, otherwise you'll burn the coffee. Mix the coffee, sugar syrup and Kahlúa and cool. Churn in an ice-cream machine, or put in the freezer, whisking every couple of hours to prevent ice crystals forming, until frozen.

GREEN TEA AND GINGER SORBET

SERVES 6–8

500ml/18fl oz/generous 2 cups
　water
3 heaped tsp green tea
　leaves, or 2 tea bags
1 small thumb of fresh ginger,
　peeled and grated
175g/6oz/generous ¾ cup
　caster (superfine) sugar
juice of ½ lemon

This is an incredibly cleansing and gentle sorbet – one for those who are technically avoiding puds but still fancy a little something sweet.

UP TO A DAY AHEAD:

Bring the water to the boil. Leave to cool for about 40 seconds and then tip over the tea leaves. Steep for 4 minutes, then strain. Whisk in the ginger, sugar and lemon juice until the sugar has dissolved, then cool.

Strain again, then churn in an ice-cream machine, or put in the freezer, whisking every couple of hours to prevent ice crystals forming, until frozen.

Jellies

There's nothing like a wibbling jelly to make faces light up around the table. And while they remind us all of a more innocent time – rabbit-shaped moulds, party hats, magicians – jellies were traditionally rather more grown-up, booze-spiked affairs.

It's entirely up to you how you play it. For largely aesthetic reasons, these jellies are served individually, though I couldn't recommend enthusiastically enough that if you do have a retro mould then you should certainly use it (always a good idea to oil it first).

As a setting agent I tend to use gelatine leaves/sheets; they seem to behave best for me, though you can happily use powdered gelatine. Make sure you use the right amount per volume of liquid, as directed on the pack. If entertaining vegetarians, then agar is a good seaweed-based setting agent.

POMEGRANATE AND PROSECCO JELLY

SERVES 6
10 gelatine leaves
1 bottle of Prosecco
300g/10½oz/1½ cups caster (superfine) sugar
seeds of 1 pomegranate

There are several ways to approach this combination. The first, fruitiest, option is to load up on pomegranate seeds and have what is essentially a bowl of pomegranate set in sparkling wine; the second involves a pinkish jelly made using a combination of Prosecco, pomegranate seeds and pomegranate juice; finally, this version favours the fizz over the fruit, settling for a golden jelly bejewelled with a few pomegranate seeds. But tweak at will.

UP TO 2 DAYS AHEAD:
Soak the gelatine in cold water for 10 minutes, then squeeze out excess water. Put the gelatine in a pan with the Prosecco and sugar and gently bring to a boil, stirring until the sugar and gelatine have dissolved. Cook just below a simmer for 5 minutes, then strain through a sieve.

Put a handful of pomegranate seeds into 6 tumblers or Champagne glasses and fill with the jelly mixture. Cover and chill until set.

DINNERTIME:
Serve as is, or with a little whipped cream.

TWEAK: For a non-alcoholic version, use pomegranate juice instead of Prosecco.

TANGERINE JELLY
WITH CANDIED PEEL

SERVES 6

6 gelatine leaves

250ml/9fl oz/generous 1 cup
water

150g/5½oz/¾ cup caster
(superfine) sugar

8 tangerines

For the candied peel

300g/10½oz/1½ cups caster
(superfine) sugar

100ml/3½fl oz/6 tbsp water

Orange jelly is the taste of childhood. It reminds me of birthday parties and slightly creepy clowns. It's my madeleine.

UP TO 2 DAYS AHEAD:

Soak the gelatine in the water for 10 minutes, then squeeze out excess water. Whisk the sugar and water together until the sugar has dissolved, then put in a pan with the gelatine. Gently bring to a boil then simmer for 3 minutes, until the gelatine has dissolved.

Peel 4 of the tangerines and discard the peel, then quarter and peel the remaining 4 – you'll need the peel of the quartered pieces for candying. Blend all the flesh thoroughly, mix with the sugar/gelatine syrup and pass through a sieve. Divide between 6 tumblers, cover and chill.

To make the candied peel, slice the peel into strips and simmer for 10 minutes in gently boiling water – this takes away the bitterness. Drain. Bring the sugar and water to a boil, stirring until the sugar has dissolved, then throw in the sliced peel. Simmer for 45 minutes – don't stir it, though you can swirl the pan if necessary – then, using a slotted spoon, lift out the peel onto a wire rack and leave until cool. Save any excess syrup for orangey cocktails, if you like. Store the candied peel in an airtight container.

DINNERTIME:

Serve the jellies topped with the candied peel.

TART: Melt some dark chocolate and dip the candied tangerine peel in it before leaving to cool.

TWEAK: Clementines, mandarins... any orangey fruit will work here. Even oranges.

STRAWBERRY AND ELDERFLOWER TRIFLE

SERVES 6

8 gelatine leaves
250ml/9fl oz/generous 1 cup
    Prosecco (or water)
100g/3½oz/½ cup caster
    (superfine) sugar
250g/9oz strawberries, hulled
    and quartered
200g/7oz savoiardi or
    ratafia biscuits
100ml/3½fl oz/7 tbsp medium-
    sweet sherry

For the custard
300ml/10fl oz/1¼ cups double
    (heavy) cream
1 vanilla pod, split
3 egg yolks
50g/1¾oz/¼ cup caster
    (superfine) sugar

To finish
300ml/10fl oz/1¼ cups double
    (heavy) cream
3 tbsp elderflower cordial

Banish any thoughts of over-whipped cream, soggy sponge and rubbery custard. When done right, this is a triumph of a pudding. There's nothing trifling about it.

8–24 HOURS AHEAD:

Soak the gelatine in cold water for 10 minutes, then squeeze out excess water. Gently warm the Prosecco, gelatine and sugar in a saucepan, stirring occasionally, until the gelatine and sugar have dissolved. Add the strawberries and cook for a further minute, then take off the heat.

Put a broken savoiardi biscuit or two into 6 large tumblers and add a good spritz of sherry to each. Top with the strawberries and pour over the jelly mixture. Cover and chill for 3–4 hours, until set.

Meanwhile, make the custard: put the cream and vanilla in a pan and slowly bring to a rolling boil. In a large heatproof bowl, whisk the egg yolks and sugar together thoroughly. When the cream is boiling, tip it directly onto the egg yolks, whisking continuously until smooth and thick. Cover and cool.

When the jelly has set, spoon over the custard, then cover and return to the fridge for at least 4 hours.

UP TO 6 HOURS AHEAD:

Whip the cream with the elderflower cordial until soft peaks form. Taste and add a little more elderflower if necessary. Cover and chill.

DINNERTIME:

Spoon the whipped cream over the custard and serve.

TART: I like the trifle *au naturel*, though there is much blinging to be done to the topping if you so wish – toasted almond flakes, a few sliced strawberries, perhaps some wild strawberries if you can find them, crystallized violets...

TWEAK: Instead of savoiardi or ratafia biscuits, use a good, slightly stale, sponge. A lemon sponge would work well.

RHUBARB, ROSE AND PISTACHIO PAVLOVA

SERVES 6

For the meringue
4 fresh egg whites
200g/7oz/1 cup caster
(superfine) sugar
For the rhubarb
400g/14oz rhubarb
100g/3½oz/½ cup caster
(superfine) sugar
juice of 1 orange
For the cream
300ml/10fl oz/1¼ cups double
(heavy) cream
50g/1¾oz/scant ½ cup icing
(confectioners') sugar
2 tsp rosewater
To finish
a handful of shelled pistachios,
roughly chopped

At its best, pavlova is the most perfect marriage of crisp and chewy meringue, soft, sweet cream and ripe fruit.

UP TO 3 DAYS AHEAD:
Preheat the oven to 120°C/250°F/Gas mark ½. Line a baking sheet with oiled baking parchment.

To make the meringue, whisk the egg whites until stiff peaks form, then whisk in the sugar, a little at a time, until glossy. Spoon 6 dollops onto the baking sheet, leaving a little space between each, and bake for 1¼ hours. Turn the oven off, leaving the meringues inside until completely cool. Store in an airtight container.

Wash the rhubarb and chop into small, even chunks. Put in a saucepan along with the sugar and orange juice, cover and cook over a medium heat for about 7–10 minutes, until the rhubarb is soft but still holds its shape for the most part. Cool and store in the fridge.

UP TO 6 HOURS AHEAD:
Whip the cream with the icing sugar and rosewater until thick and glossy, then cover and chill.

DINNERTIME:
Put a small blob of cream on each plate to stop the pudding sliding around and top with a meringue. Top the meringues with a spoonful of rhubarb and a good dollop of cream. Finish with chopped pistachios and serve.

TART: If you can get hold of dried rose petals, these would add a final flourish of colour.
TWEAK: Orange and rhubarb being such happy bedfellows, you could swap the rosewater for orange blossom water, or even grated orange zest.
TOMORROW: Leftover rhubarb is a pretty unbeatable breakfast accompaniment.

GOAT'S CURD CREMETS WITH STRAWBERRIES, LAMBRUSCO AND BASIL

The credit for this dish lies entirely at Lucas Hollweg's brilliant feet. It was one of those 'er, OK' moments when he suggested doing a goat's curd cremets for pudding at the supper club, but it was – like everything else he cooks – utterly delicious. Think roughly along the lines of cheesecake meets panna cotta, but with the soft, earthy tang you get from goat's milk.

You can find goat's curd in some cheese shops and even supermarkets, though it's easy to make – tip a tub of goat's milk yogurt into a sieve lined with muslin (cheesecloth) or a tea towel and leave for a day or two to strain out all the whey.

SERVES 6

2 gelatine leaves
1 vanilla pod
250g/9oz goat's curd
50g/1¾oz/scant ½ cup icing
    (confectioners') sugar
zest of ½ lemon
250ml/9fl.oz/generous 1 cup
    double (heavy) creams
300g/10½oz strawberries,
    hulled and quartered
50g/1¾oz/¼ cup caster
    (superfine) sugar
150ml/5fl oz/⅔ cup Lambrusco
    or other red wine
a handful of small basil leaves
    (Greek basil is ideal)

6–24 HOURS AHEAD:

Soak the gelatine in cold water for 10 minutes, squeeze out excess water, then dissolve in 3 tbsp simmering water. Leave to cool for 10 minutes. Meanwhile, split the vanilla pod and scrape out the seeds onto the goat's curd. Mix with the icing sugar and lemon zest. Strain the gelatinous water onto the goat's curd and beat through, along with the cream.

Line 6 ramekins with clingfilm or – better – muslin (this creates a lovely texture) and spoon in the goat's curd mixture. Cover and chill overnight.

2 HOURS AHEAD:

Mix the strawberries with the sugar and Lambrusco and leave to macerate.

DINNERTIME:

Turn the cremets out onto serving plates and spoon over the strawberries. Tear some basil over the top and serve.

TART: To make it more cheesecakey, you could line the bottom of the ramekins with crushed digestive biscuits.
TWEAK: If goat's curd is a bridge too far, then you could use very thick yogurt, or cream cheese.

EXPLODING CHOCOLATE POTS

SERVES 6

450ml/16fl oz/scant 2 cups double (heavy) cream
200g/7oz dark chocolate, broken up
50g/1¾oz milk chocolate, broken up
3 tbsp brandy
2 egg yolks
¼ tsp sea salt
2 tbsp popping candy

These are a bit of fun, really. The explosion comes from the popping candy added at the end, which I won't pretend adds much to the flavour, but it certainly perks up your standard chocolate pudding.

4–24 HOURS AHEAD:

Slowly bring the cream to a boil, then take off the heat. Add all the chocolate and stir. Leave until melted, then stir thoroughly until smooth. Leave to cool for 5 minutes, then stir through the brandy, egg yolks and salt. Divide between 6 ramekins, cover and chill until dinnertime.

DINNERTIME:

Top with a sprinkling of popping candy and serve.

TART: Add 100ml/3½fl oz/7 tbsp very strong coffee to the chocolate along with the brandy.
TWEAK: Omit the brandy if you prefer, or use an orange liqueur such as Grand Marnier instead.

NEW ORLEANS BREAD PUDDING
WITH WHISKEY SAUCE

SERVES 6–8 (POSSIBLY 10, DEPENDING ON WHAT YOU'VE ALREADY EATEN)

300g/10½oz dark chocolate, broken up

300ml/10fl oz/1¼ cups double (heavy) cream

300ml/10fl oz/1¼ cups whole milk

1 vanilla pod, split

6 egg yolks

150g/5½oz/¾ cup caster (superfine) sugar

3 tbsp Frangelico hazelnut liqueur (optional)

100g/3½oz/7 tbsp butter, softened

400g/14oz slightly stale baguette, sliced

a good handful of chocolate chips

For the whiskey sauce

150g/5½oz/generous ½ cup butter

200g/7oz/1 cup dark brown sugar

150ml/5fl oz/⅔ cup double (heavy) cream

100ml/3½fl oz/7 tbsp bourbon or rye

On his return from the New Orleans Jazz Festival, my friend Edu phoned immediately to rhapsodize about the food he'd eaten, from alligator po'boys to gumbo and back around. But it was bread pudding that most enthused him – sticky, chocolatey, bread pudding. I'm not sure the actual words he used are printable, but suffice to say the Louisiana version of bread and butter pudding is a winner.

UP TO A DAY AHEAD:

Preheat the oven to 150°C/300°F/Gas mark 2.

Melt the chocolate in a heatproof bowl over a pan of barely simmering water. Meanwhile, put the cream, milk and vanilla pod in a pan and slowly bring to a boil. In a large heatproof bowl, whisk the egg yolks and caster sugar together until pale and light, then tip the cream directly onto them, whisking furiously. Leave to cool for a couple of minutes, then fold through the melted chocolate and the Frangelico, if using. Discard the vanilla pod.

Butter the bread on both sides and rub an ovenproof dish with butter. Push a layer of bread into the dish and scatter with chocolate chips, then pour over some of the chocolate custard. Repeat in layers until you've used all the bread, and tip over any remaining custard and chocolate chips. Bake for 1 hour.

To make the whiskey sauce, melt the butter and sugar together and simmer gently for a couple of minutes. Add the cream and bourbon and simmer for 15 minutes, then set aside. Cool and chill both items.

1 HOUR AHEAD:

Preheat the oven to 120°C/250°F/Gas mark ½.

Put the bread pudding back in the oven for 30 minutes to heat through. Gently warm the whiskey sauce over a low heat.

DINNERTIME:

Serve the bread pudding with a good dousing of whiskey sauce.

TWEAK: For a more British version, leave the chocolate out of the custard, and use malt loaf instead of baguette.

STICKY APPLE CAKE WITH DRUNK CURRANTS

SERVES 6–8

250g/9oz/ generous 1 cup butter, softened
100g/3½oz/½ cup molasses or dark brown sugar
2–3 apples, peeled, cored and sliced
150g/5½oz/¾ cup soft light brown sugar
2 eggs, lightly beaten
250g/9oz/2 cups self-raising flour
2 tsp ground cinnamon
¼ tsp ground allspice
a pinch of salt
crème fraîche, to serve

For the currants
100g/3½oz/½ cup caster (superfine) sugar
150ml/5fl oz/⅔ cup dark rum
100g/3½oz/generous ½ cup currants

This is a sort of Anglo-French number, a marriage between a tarte Tatin and good old-fashioned cake. Served with currants that have been to Jamaica for their holidays.

UP TO 3 DAYS AHEAD:

Preheat the oven to 180°C/350°F/Gas mark 4. Grease a 20cm/8in diameter cake tin.

Melt 50g/1¾oz/4 tbsp of the butter in a small saucepan, add the molasses sugar and stir until dissolved. Gently simmer until rich and dark, then tip into the cake tin. Arrange the apple slices on top.

Beat the light brown sugar and the remaining butter together until light and fluffy, then beat in the eggs, a little at a time. Fold in the flour, spices and salt and spread over the apples. Bake for 35–40 minutes, until springy to the touch. Leave to cool in the tin.

For the boozy currants, mix the caster sugar and rum in a small pan, add the currants and simmer gently for 10 minutes, then set aside.

15 MINUTES AHEAD:

Gently warm the cake in a low oven, if you fancy, though it's just as good served cold. Warm the currants over a gentle heat.

DINNERTIME:

Turn the cake out onto a plate, slice and serve with a blob of crème fraîche and a spoonful of currants.

FLOURLESS
CHOCOLATE CAKE

SERVES 6–8

150g/5½oz/generous ½ cup
   butter, softened
200g/7oz dark chocolate,
   broken up
150g/5½oz/¾ cup caster
   (superfine) sugar
4 eggs, separated
150g/5½oz/generous 1½ cups
   ground almonds
To serve
cocoa powder
single (light) cream

It seems an increasing number of people are finding themselves at odds with wheat. Some find it bloats them, others that it knots their bellies. Quite handy, then, to have a cake up your sleeve that doesn't require any flour.

UP TO 2 DAYS AHEAD:

Preheat the oven to 220°C/425°F/Gas mark 7. Line the bottom of a 20cm/8in diameter cake tin with greaseproof paper. Give the sides a little rub with butter.

Melt the chocolate in a heatproof bowl over a pan of barely simmering water. When the chocolate has fully melted, leave to cool for a minute or two. Meanwhile, beat the butter and sugar together until light and fluffy, then beat in the egg yolks. Fold in the ground almonds. Fold the cooled melted chocolate through the mixture.

In a clean bowl, beat the egg whites until stiff peaks form. Very gently fold the whites through the cake mixture. Carefully tip into the cake tin and bake for 20 minutes.

Remove from the oven and leave to cool completely.

UP TO A DAY AHEAD:

When the cake is completely cool, run a palette knife around the edge of the cake tin, and turn out onto a plate. Cover.

DINNERTIME:

Dust the cake with cocoa powder and serve with cream.

TART: Mix a handful of chopped hazelnuts and the grated zest of 1 orange through the mixture along with the almonds.
TWEAK: If catering for someone with a nut allergy but no wheat intolerance, use flour instead of ground almonds.

TREACLE TART

SERVES 6–8

For the pastry

100g/3½oz/7 tbsp butter,
    cubed and chilled
200g/7oz/generous 1½ cups
    plain (all-purpose) flour
½ tsp salt
2 eggs

For the filling

450g/1lb golden syrup
100g/3½oz/2 cups fresh
    breadcrumbs
zest of 1 lemon
1 egg, lightly beaten
1 tsp sea salt

The treacle tarts at school had a reputation for being the scourge of the hard-working dentist. Those that didn't stick for days in your teeth would break them outright, and any that were vaguely edible were so sweet that they'd rot your molars on their way down. I *think* this recipe avoids these perils, with a good tang of lemon and a filling that isn't as brittle as an overbaked flapjack.

UP TO 2 DAYS AHEAD:

To make the pastry, rub the butter into the flour with your fingertips and thumbs (or in a food processor) until it resembles breadcrumbs, then add the salt and 1 egg and mix to form a dough. If it's too dry, add a little splash of cold water. Wrap in clingfilm and chill in the freezer for 10 minutes, or in the fridge for 30 minutes (or longer if necessary).

On a lightly floured surface, roll out the pastry and line a 24cm/9½in tart tin. Put it back in the freezer for 10 minutes or fridge for 30 minutes. Preheat the oven to 160°C/325°F/Gas mark 3.

Line the pastry shell with baking parchment and tip in something to weigh it down – baking beans, dried chickpeas, the contents of your piggy bank – then bake for 25 minutes. Remove from the oven and remove the baking beans and parchment. Brush the pastry with beaten egg and bake for a further 5 minutes. Remove from the oven and turn it down to 140°C/275°F/Gas mark 1.

To make the filling, mix the golden syrup (use a spatula to make sure you get every drop out of the tin), breadcrumbs, lemon zest, egg and salt, and tip into the pastry shell. Bake for 50 minutes to 1 hour, until set. Cool and cover.

30 MINUTES AHEAD (OPTIONAL):

Preheat the oven to 120°C/250°F/Gas mark ½ and gently warm the tart through.

DINNERTIME:

Serve the treacle tart warm or cold, with clotted cream or vanilla ice cream.

TART: Ginger works particularly well here, either in the form of ½ tsp ground ginger, or some finely chopped crystallized ginger.
TWEAK: For a darker, richer tart, replace 100g/3½oz of the golden syrup with black treacle.
TOMORROW: Store in the fridge. Eat at will.

RICE PUDDING

SERVES 6–8

25g/1oz/2 tbsp unsalted butter
850ml/1½ pints/3½ cups whole milk
1 vanilla pod, split
100g/3½oz/½ cup pudding (short-grain) rice
zest of ½ lemon
nutmeg
3 tbsp caster (superfine) sugar
100ml/3½fl oz/7 tbsp double (heavy) cream

Ah, the great divider of men. Skin or no skin? To jam or not to jam? And that's for people who actually *like* rice pudding. For many it's far too redolent of school dinners and long afternoons spent staring at an increasingly congealed mass, back when children were forced to finish what was on their plate instead of quite reasonably stopping when they were full. If you're one of these hapless souls, then I urge you to reconsider rice pudding. Few puds are simpler, or more cosseting.

UP TO 6 HOURS AHEAD:

Preheat the oven to 150°C/300°F/Gas mark 2. Butter an oven-proof dish.

Put the milk and vanilla in a saucepan and slowly bring to just below a boil.

Meanwhile, rinse the rice under cold running water and tip into the dish. Add a few knobs of butter, the lemon zest, a little grating of fresh nutmeg and the sugar. Pour in the milk and stir. Bake for 1 hour, stirring after 30 minutes.

Stir in the cream and cook for another 15 minutes. Serve, or cool and chill.

30 MINUTES AHEAD:

Preheat the oven to 150°C/300°F/Gas mark 2, and gently warm the pudding through.

DINNERTIME:

Serve with jam, or extra cream, or whatever you fancy.

TART: Nigel Slater puts a bay leaf in his rice pudding, which adds a subtle, aromatic, savoury note.
TWEAK: Try it with orange instead of lemon zest.

PEAR AND ALMOND TART

SERVES 6–8

For the pastry

100g/3½oz/7 tbsp butter, cubed and chilled

200g/7oz/generous 1½ cups plain (all-purpose) flour

zest of 1 lemon

a pinch of salt

50–100ml/2–3½fl oz/3–7 tbsp cold vodka or water

1 egg yolk, beaten with a little water

For the pears

500g/1lb 2oz/2½ cups caster (superfine) sugar

1 litre/1¾ pints/4 cups water

200ml/7fl oz/generous ¾ cup amaretto (optional)

1 cinnamon stick

1 star anise

4 pears

For the filling

100g/3½oz/½ cup caster (superfine) sugar

100g/3½oz/7 tbsp butter, softened

2 eggs

50g/1¾oz/7 tbsp self-raising flour

100g/3½oz/1 cup ground almonds

a pinch of salt

The use of vodka in pastry has been a complete revelation to me. It has nothing to do with flavour and everything to do with the alcohol, which both arrests gluten development and evaporates more easily, leaving you with crisp, flaky pastry.

UP TO 3 DAYS AHEAD:

To make the pastry, rub the cold butter into the flour with your fingertips and thumbs (or in a food processor) until it resembles breadcrumbs. Mix through the lemon zest and salt, then add the vodka or water – not all at once – kneading lightly and adding more liquid until the mixture comes together. Form into a ball, wrap in clingfilm and chill for 30 minutes in the fridge, or 10 minutes in the freezer.

On a lightly floured surface, roll out the pastry and line a 24cm/9½in tart tin. Put it back in the freezer for 10 minutes or fridge for 30 minutes. Preheat the oven to 160°C/325°F/Gas mark 3.

Line the pastry shell with baking parchment and tip in something to weigh it down – baking beans, dried chickpeas – then bake for 25 minutes. Remove from the oven and remove the baking beans and parchment. Brush the pastry with the beaten egg yolk. Bake for a further 5 minutes. Remove and cool. Set aside until needed.

For the pears, put the sugar, water, amaretto and spices in a large pan and bring to a boil, stirring until the sugar has dissolved. Simmer gently while you peel the pears. Add them to the pan and poach for 1 hour. Remove the pears and cool. Continue to simmer the liquid for a further 30–40 minutes until reduced and syrupy. Quarter and core the pears, then halve the quarters again. Cover and chill.

When ready to bake, preheat the oven to 180°C/350°F/Gas mark 4. Beat the sugar and butter together until pale and fluffy, then beat in the eggs, one at a time. Fold in the flour, ground almonds and salt, then spread in the pastry shell. Top with the slices of pear and brush with the spiced syrup. Bake for 45 minutes. Brush again with the syrup, cool, cover and chill, or serve warm.

45 MINUTES AHEAD (OPTIONAL):

Preheat the oven to 160°C/325°F/Gas mark 3, and gently warm the tart through.

DINNERTIME:

Serve the tart warm or cold, with crème fraîche, single cream or ice cream.

TART: A few toasted flaked almonds, scattered over the tart before serving, would be a nice touch.

TWEAK: A simplified version: buy ready-made pastry and canned pears, simmering the syrup from the can with extra water, sugar and spices.

Little sweet things

It's funny how even at the end of a dinner of Churchillian proportions you can almost always find a corner of your belly into which to tuck something sweet – the thinnest of chocolate mints, or the ambassador's favourite chocolate and hazelnut confection. I am never one to refuse a Malteser. But to think that a friend had bothered to spend an extra half hour putting together one more morsel with which to send me off into the night will only endear them to me further.

Some of these recipes don't have a 'tart' section. Please don't think me lazy, but in these cases it's because I feel they're quite tarty enough already.

In do-ahead terms, they can all be done several days in advance, and many freeze well too.

CHOCOLATE TRUFFLES

MAKES ABOUT 15 TRUFFLES

150ml/5fl oz/2/3 cup double
(heavy) cream
100g/3½oz dark chocolate
50g/1¾oz milk chocolate
1 tbsp brandy (optional)
2 tbsp unsweetened cocoa
powder

These are my standard sweet things for the supper club. Even the most ham-fisted, harassed cook couldn't mess them up, and they can easily be done while you've got three other things on the go. Most importantly, they are delicious, and if you can casually drop a plate of homemade truffles as rich, dense and chocolatey as these on the table then your friends will think you a quiet genius.

UP TO 5 DAYS AHEAD:

Put the cream in a small saucepan over a low heat and slowly bring to a boil. Meanwhile, smash up the chocolate. When the cream is just about to boil, take it off the heat and throw in the chocolate pieces. Leave to melt for 5–10 minutes, then stir the brandy through vigorously until smooth and glossy. Cover and chill.

Remove from the fridge and, when softened a little, use two teaspoons to shape the mixture into evenly sized balls. Roll between your hands for neatly shaped truffles – though I tend to squidge them into something more rustic – then toss in the cocoa powder. Store in the fridge in an airtight container.

TART: Add ½ tsp chilli powder along with the brandy for a good kick. A pinch of sea salt never hurts, either.

TWEAK: Play around with liqueurs instead of the brandy – Grand Marnier, Kahlúa or Frangelico all work well.

FLORENTINES

MAKES 12

vegetable oil for brushing

2 tsp plain (all-purpose) flour,
    plus some for dusting

15g/½oz/1 tbsp butter

3 tbsp caster (superfine) sugar

2 tbsp double (heavy) cream

75g/2¾oz/¾ cup flaked
    (slivered) almonds

2 tbsp chopped candied peel

2 tbsp chopped glacé
    cherries

a pinch of sea salt

50g/1¾oz dark chocolate

My first encounter with Florentines was at Bettys Tea Rooms in Harrogate with my American aunt Rita. It seemed to me then that she'd made the trip from the States purely in order to get her hands on a Florentine, such was her excitement about a pilgrimage to that anachronistic little tea room. At about that same time – I suppose I was four or five – I believed that Rita and I were able to communicate telepathically across the Atlantic. Assuming this is still the case, a written dedication to her would be unnecessary, but just in case the reception is poor, this one's for you Aunt Rita.

UP TO 3 DAYS AHEAD:

Preheat the oven to 160°C/325°F/Gas mark 3. Line a couple of baking sheets with baking parchment, brush with vegetable oil and dust with flour.

Melt the butter in a saucepan, add the sugar and flour and stir until smooth. Add the cream and stir to combine, then take off the heat and stir in the almonds, chopped fruit and salt. Spoon onto the baking sheets, a teaspoon at a time and leaving a decent gap between each. Flatten slightly with the back of the spoon, then bake for 15–20 minutes, until golden. You may need to do this in two batches.

Meanwhile, break up the chocolate and melt in a heatproof bowl over a pan of barely simmering water.

Put the baked Florentines, upside down, on a wire rack and brush the flat undersides with the melted chocolate. Leave until cool, and store in an airtight container.

BROWNIES

MAKES 20

200g/7oz/generous ¾ cup
    unsalted butter
200g/7oz dark chocolate,
    broken up
3 eggs
250g/9oz/1¼ cups caster
    (superfine) sugar
1 tsp vanilla extract
125g/4½oz/1 cup plain
    (all-purpose) flour
50g/1¾oz/½ cup chopped
    walnuts
a good pinch of salt

These are, I realize, just puddings in miniature. But there's something about little brownies that is somehow seductive. Perhaps it's because you don't think they 'count', being only really very small and innocent. They're quite handy, too, for a meal where you don't feel the need to serve pudding but still fancy something sweet at the end.

UP TO 3 DAYS AHEAD:

Preheat the oven to 180°C/350°F/Gas mark 4. Line a baking tin, approximately 27 x 20cm/11 x 8in, with greaseproof paper.

Melt the butter and chocolate in a heatproof bowl over a pan of barely simmering water. Meanwhile, beat together the eggs and sugar with the vanilla extract. When light and pale, beat in the melted chocolate. Fold in the flour, walnuts and salt, and tip into the baking tin. Bake for 30 minutes, or until firm on top. It should still be good and moist, so the clean skewer test is no use here. Leave to cool in the tin.

Cut into small pieces and store in an airtight container.

TART: The child in me can't resist the idea of adding white chocolate buttons to the mixture along with the walnuts.
TWEAK: Omit the walnuts if you prefer.

BAKLAVA

MAKES 20

400g/14oz/2 cups caster (superfine) sugar
250ml/9fl oz/generous 1 cup water
juice of ½ lemon
1 tbsp orange blossom water
20 sheets of filo pastry
200g/7oz/generous ¾ cup butter, melted
300g/10½oz/2½ cups shelled pistachios, roughly ground

This Middle Eastern confection comes in many guises, though the common theme is their finger-gluing stickiness and intense sweetness. They are best served, therefore, with something strong and bitter like coffee.

UP TO 3 DAYS AHEAD:

First make the syrup: put the sugar and water in a pan over a low heat and stir until the sugar has dissolved. Turn up the heat and bring to a boil. Simmer for 10 minutes until thick and syrupy. Take off the heat and add the lemon juice and orange blossom water. Leave to cool.

Preheat the oven to 150°C/300°F/Gas mark 2. You can use a small baking sheet or 20cm/8in diameter cake tin; trim the pastry sheets so they're about 1cm/½in wider than the baking sheet or cake tin. Lay 10 sheets of filo pastry in the tin, brushing each sheet thoroughly with melted butter. Spread over the ground pistachios, keeping back a small handful, and then top with the remaining sheets of filo, again brushing each with butter.

Using a sharp knife, cut the baklava into about 20 squares or diamonds. Bake for 1 hour. Remove from the oven and pour over the syrup. Sprinkle a little of the remaining pistachios in the centre of each piece. Leave to cool. Remove from the tin and store in an airtight container.

TWEAK: Pistachios are quite expensive, so you could replace half of them with ground walnuts.

ROSE
MARSHMALLOWS

MAKES 50

4 tbsp icing (confectioners')
    sugar
4 tbsp cornflour (cornstarch)
vegetable oil for brushing
10 gelatine leaves
400ml/14fl oz/scant 1¾ cups
    water
500g/1lb 2oz/2½ cups caster
    (superfine) sugar
2 tbsp rosewater
2 large egg whites

Of all the petits fours I've served at the supper club, these have perhaps got the best reaction. For one thing, nobody can quite believe you've made marshmallows yourself, though in truth they're incredibly straightforward. This makes quite a lot, but they'll keep a good while – perfect for bonfire night.

UP TO 3 DAYS AHEAD:

Mix the icing sugar and cornflour. Oil a 20 x 30cm/8 x 12in baking sheet and thoroughly dust with some of the icing sugar and cornflour mixture.

Soak the gelatine in 150ml/5fl oz/⅔ cup of the water for 10 minutes. Meanwhile, put the remaining water, the caster sugar and rosewater in a saucepan and whisk over a low heat until the sugar has dissolved, then bring to a boil and simmer for 15 minutes: the temperature should reach 127°C/260°F on a sugar thermometer, or, when a drop of the liquid is added to cold water, it should form a soft ball. Add the gelatine and its water. Simmer for another 2 minutes, until the gelatine has dissolved, then strain into a jug.

Whisk the egg whites until stiff, then slowly pour in the gelatine mixture while continuing to whisk. Keep whisking for a good 10 minutes until the mixture is thick and glossy, then tip into the prepared baking sheet. Chill for a couple of hours until set.

Dust a chopping board with the remaining icing sugar and cornflour mixture. Run a knife around the edge of the marshmallow to loosen, then tip onto the chopping board. Cut into squares and roll in the sugar, then leave on a wire rack to dry for a few hours. Store in an airtight container.

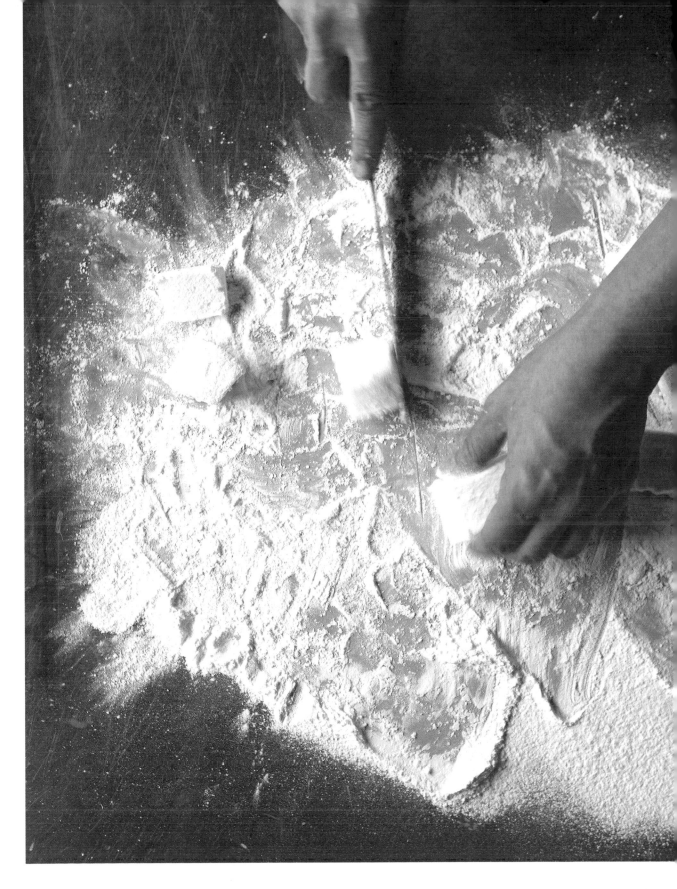

SALTED CARAMEL CHOCOLATE

SERVES 6–8

vegetable oil for brushing
200g/7oz dark chocolate
100g/3½oz milk chocolate
75g/2¾oz/5 tbsp butter
125g/4½oz/generous ½ cup
   soft brown sugar
1 tsp sea salt
100ml/3½fl oz/7 tbsp double
   (heavy) cream

The credit for this naughty slab must go to my wife Rosie, who, along with two friends, took over the supper club for their own night, Pigs in Pinnies. I merely sat and gleefully ate. And ate and ate.
   Serve fridge cold. Ideally with a hammer.

UP TO 2 DAYS AHEAD:

Lightly oil a small baking sheet or dish and put it in the freezer.

Smash up the chocolate and put it in a heatproof bowl. Place over a pan of barely simmering water and melt, stirring occasionally. When melted, tip onto the chilled baking sheet and refrigerate until set.

Melt the butter in a saucepan and add the sugar and salt. Stir until the sugar has dissolved, then add the cream. Simmer for 10 minutes, stirring occasionally, until thick and sticky. Pour all over the chocolate. Leave to cool, then return to the fridge until ready to serve.

To serve, smash up with whatever you have to hand and put the shards on a chilled plate.

TWEAK: Don't muck about with melting and resetting chocolate, and just pour your caramel over a big slab of dark chocolate.

MINI MERINGUES

MAKES 12–15

vegetable oil for brushing
2 egg whites
100g/3½oz/½ cup caster (superfine) sugar
100ml/3½fl oz/6 tbsp double (heavy) cream
1 tbsp icing (confectioners') sugar
¼ tsp vanilla extract
150g/5½oz blueberries

A very handy recipe for when you've got a few egg whites kicking about. It requires little effort, and the meringues freeze quite merrily.

UP TO 3 DAYS AHEAD:

Preheat the oven to 150°C/300°F/Gas mark 2. Line a baking sheet with baking parchment and brush lightly with oil.

Whisk the egg whites until stiff, then whisk in the caster sugar, a little at a time. Continue to whisk until stiff and glossy. Using a teaspoon, put 24–30 spoonfuls of meringue mix on the baking sheet. Put in the oven and cook for 5 minutes. Turn the oven off but leave the meringues in there until the oven is completely cool.

UP TO 4 HOURS AHEAD:

Whip the cream until thick, then add the icing sugar and vanilla. Keep whisking until thick.

1 HOUR AHEAD:

Take a meringue and put a good blob of cream on the underside. Stick a blueberry into the cream and then squidge together with the bottom of another meringue. Repeat for the remaining meringues. Store in the fridge in an airtight container.

TART: Fold a little raspberry or cherry cordial through the meringue mixture when stiff.
TWEAK: Instead of blueberries, use another small fruit – wild strawberries would be terrific.

CANTUCCINI

MAKES ABOUT 30 BISCUITS
250g/9oz/2 cups plain
    (all-purpose) flour
150g/5½oz/¾ cup granulated
    sugar
½ tsp baking powder
¼ tsp salt
zest and juice of ½ orange
zest and juice of ½ lemon
2 eggs, lightly beaten
¼ tsp vanilla extract
150g/5½oz/1 cup almonds
    (skin on)

These Tuscan treats are deceptively simple – there's no great art to their creation, instead more of a chuck it all together act. The dough, you should be warned, is very sticky. Don't fret. Pretend you're at playschool.

This recipe is based on the one in Susan McKenna Grant's beautiful *Piano Piano Pieno* (HarperCollins, 2006).

UP TO A WEEK AHEAD:

Preheat the oven to 200°C/400°F/Gas mark 6. Line a baking sheet with lightly floured greaseproof paper.

Mix the flour, sugar, baking powder and salt in a large bowl and make a well in the centre. Throw in the orange and lemon juice and zest, eggs and vanilla, and mix together thoroughly. Now briefly knead through the almonds.

With lightly floured hands, divide the dough into two pieces and roll into slightly flattened sausage shapes. Transfer to the baking sheet and bake for 20 minutes.

Remove from the oven and cool for 5 minutes, then slice at an angle. Lay the cantuccini flat on the sheet and bake for a further 10 minutes. Cool and store in airtight containers.

Tuscans serve these with cold vin santo. You could, too.

DATE BALLS

MAKES 20
125g/4½oz/generous ½ cup
    butter
175g/6oz/generous ¾ cup
    caster (superfine) sugar
200g/7oz/1½ cups stoned
    dates, finely chopped
1 egg, beaten
1 tbsp milk
1 tsp vanilla extract
½ tsp salt
a small handful of chopped
    nuts (optional)
50g/1¾oz/2 cups rice crispies
a handful of desiccated
    coconut

These are a particularly American treat, which my mum makes every Christmas.

UP TO A WEEK AHEAD:

Melt the butter in a saucepan and add the sugar and the dates. Stir and bring to a gentle boil. Simmer for a minute or two, then take off the heat. Stir through the egg, milk, vanilla and salt and mix until smooth, then add the nuts, if using, and the rice crispies. Set aside until cool.

Form into small balls and roll in desiccated coconut. Store in an airtight container.

Drinks

A sharpener, a loosener, a refresher or a bracer, a good cocktail can start the evening off like nothing else. It's not, I should clarify, about getting your guests hammered. If you've spent time cooking dinner, then you don't want everyone to sit down and faceplant in the soup. But it's a terrific way of taking the edge off a long day or week, as well as oiling the social wheels – particularly useful if some guests don't know each other.

Most of the drinks in this section can be mixed ahead and chilled for a good few hours.

NEGRONI

FOR 1 COCKTAIL
50ml/1¾fl oz gin
25ml/scant 1fl oz Martini rosso
25ml/scant 1fl oz Campari
ice
a twist of orange peel

The best nights begin with a negroni or two. It is, as far as I'm concerned, the king of cocktails, unbeatable in its efficacy, heady in flavour and herbal in aroma, and, with the possible exception of a Martini, unparalleled in its ability to perk one up with a single sip.

I favour these measurements, though some go for equal measures, in which case 35ml/1¼fl oz of each should suffice.

AHEAD:
Mix the gin, Martini and Campari. Chill.

TO SERVE:
Fill a tumbler with ice and pour over the negroni. Garnish with a twist of orange peel and serve.

MULLED CIDER

SERVES 6
1 litre/1¾ pints/4 cups cider or apple juice
200ml/7fl oz/generous ¾ cup brandy, dark rum or whisky (optional)
200ml/7fl oz/generous ¾ cup water
200g/7oz/1 cup caster (superfine) sugar
2 star anise
2 cinnamon sticks
2 cloves
a piece of orange peel
a piece of lemon peel

A good Christmas cocktail, and far preferable to mulled wine in my opinion. Use apple juice instead of cider for a virgin version.

AHEAD:
Put all the ingredients in a large saucepan and warm through, stirring to dissolve the sugar. If making in advance, warm for 30 minutes just below a boil, then leave to infuse.

TO SERVE:
Bring to just below a boil and serve in sturdy heatproof glasses.

MOSCOW MULE

SERVES 4
150ml/5fl oz/⅔ cup vodka
juice of 2 limes
a few shakes of Angostura bitters
ice
800ml/1½ pints/generous 3¼ cups ginger beer

This is the drink we most regularly serve guests at the Secret Larder, for the simple reason that it's a near-guaranteed, if not particularly refined, crowd-pleaser and is a cinch to make.

AHEAD:
Mix the vodka, lime juice and bitters. Chill.

TO SERVE:
Fill 4 tall (highball) glasses with ice. Add the vodka and lime potion. Top up with ginger beer. Serve, with a wedge of lime if you like.

RASPBERRY GIN AND TONIC

SERVES 2 HITCHENS/PARKERS
(OR 4 IF YOU DON'T WANT TO
SEE DOUBLE)
125g/4½oz raspberries
juice of ½ lemon
1 tbsp caster (superfine) sugar
200ml/7fl oz/generous
    ¾ cup gin
ice
tonic water, preferably cans
lemon slices, to garnish

'Observe the same rule to all gin drinks,' wrote Christopher Hitchens (though I think he may have borrowed the line from Dorothy Parker), 'that you would in judging breasts: one is far too few, and three is one too many.' This recipe comes with a disclaimer – it is sweet and moreish and ever so easy to overdo. But one might not be quite enough.

AHEAD:
Blend the raspberries, lemon juice and sugar and pass through a sieve. Mix this juice with the gin. Chill.

TO SERVE:
Fill 2 (or 4) tall glasses with ice and put a quarter of the raspberry gin mix in each. Top up with tonic water and garnish with a slice of lemon. Repeat if necessary.

WHITE RUSSIAN

SERVES 4
200ml/7fl oz/generous
    ¾ cup vodka
100ml/3½fl oz/7 tbsp coffee
    liqueur (Kahlúa or Tia Maria)
150ml/5fl oz/2/3 cup
    whole milk
ice

White Russians are infamously known as the preferred libation of Jeff Bridges' Dude in *The Big Lebowski*. When I first saw the film, I wondered why on earth anyone would want to put cream in a cocktail. And then I lived in Moscow and it all made sense – bad vodka could be masked with coffee and cream, or conversely off cream could be hidden by alcohol and blind faith. I prefer a lighter version, using milk instead, though if it's a particularly harsh winter then cream it is.

AHEAD:
Mix the vodka, coffee liqueur and milk. Chill.

TO SERVE:
Fill 4 tumblers with ice and pour the White Russian over the top.

MICHELADA, ALMOST

SERVES 4
5 tbsp tequila (optional)
juice of 2 limes
a few shakes of Tabasco
    (to taste)
a few shakes of Worcestershire
    sauce
salt and pepper
ice
4 bottles of beer – a good-
    quality lager or IPA

When Tom Parker Bowles, author of the magnificent *Let's Eat* (Pavilion, 2012), came to do a Mexican-themed evening at the supper club, this is the cocktail he suggested. It is, I suppose, Mexico's punchy answer to shandy, or perhaps even to a Bloody Mary, though Tom's version omitted tomato juice. At any rate, the combination of beer, tequila, lime juice and Tabasco is as good a way of pushing off from the shore as I know.

AHEAD:
Mix the tequila (it using), lime juice, Tabasco and Worcestershire sauce, and add a good pinch of salt and twist of pepper. Chill.

TO SERVE:
Fill 4 tall glasses with ice and divide the Tabasco mix among them. Top up with beer and serve.

SAZERAC

SERVES 4
4 tsp caster (superfine) sugar
a few good shakes of
    Peychaud's Bitters
200ml/7fl oz/generous ¾ cup
    rye whiskey or bourbon
ice
a splash of absinthe or Pernod
4 pieces of lemon peel

This is the official cocktail of New Orleans, which is an endorsement in itself. Stick on some Fats Domino and break out the bitters. In Louisiana it would be Peychaud's, but Angostura bitters will do the job.

AHEAD:
Mix the sugar, bitters and whiskey until the sugar has dissolved. Chill.

TO SERVE:
Fill a cocktail shaker with ice and pour in a splash of absinthe or Pernod. Give it a good shake, then discard the liquid. Add the whiskey mix and shake again. Fill 4 tumblers with ice and add the mixture. Garnish with a twist of lemon peel and serve.

PROPER SNAKEBITE

SERVES 4
2 cold bottles of dry cider
2 cold bottles of beer – an
    American IPA works well
crème de cassis

In 2001 former US President Bill Clinton had the pleasure of visiting my local town of Harrogate in North Yorkshire. Shunning the genteel and overpriced Bettys Tea Rooms, he opted instead for the Old Bell Tavern, where he ordered a snakebite, only to be told by the landlord that they were illegal. Supposedly, rowdy drinkers would get tanked up on this mixture of beer and cider, scuffles would ensue, and really it was just not worth the landlord's bother. They're not really illegal, but that's Yorkshire for you – ex-President or plumber, rules are rules.

Pour equal parts cider and lager into 4 chilled glasses. Add a dash of cassis. Serve.

WHISKY MAC

SERVES 1
50ml/1¾fl oz whisky
35ml/1¼fl oz ginger wine

The whisky Macdonald barely needs a full recipe, though a pre-amble should perhaps mention that using anything but a Scotch whisky is approaching sacrilegious, as is using a single malt – a blend is fine for these purposes. It's ideal for a chilly evening. Oh, and while a possibly alien ingredient, you should be able to find ginger wine in any supermarket, off-licence or wine shop.

Mix. Serve. No ice.

APPLE, CUCUMBER, ELDERFLOWER AND MINT VIRGIN COCKTAIL

SERVES 4

400ml/14fl oz/scant 1¾ cups
    clear apple juice
juice of 1 lemon
2 tbsp elderflower cordial
ice
soda water
4 shards of cucumber
a few sprigs of mint
lemon segments

Here's a fresh and lively virgin cocktail for when alcohol doesn't appeal. And if it does, then a slug of vodka or gin would be just the thing.

AHEAD:
Mix the apple juice, lemon juice and elderflower cordial. Chill.

TO SERVE:
Fill 4 tall glasses with ice and divide the apple juice mix between them. Top up with soda water, garnish with cucumber, mint and lemon, and serve.

Menu suggestions

These are merely ideas and recommendations, some based on menus I've cooked at the Secret Larder, some based on a particular theme, and some are simply dishes I think work well together, both in terms of flavours and textures and in terms of making things easy for you when serving.

There is of course no need to do the full menu if for whatever reason it doesn't fit your particular bill. Ultimately it's your dinner...

A SPRING MENU
Radishes with butter and salt (p.31)
Chilled pea and courgette soup
    with yogurt and harissa (p.56)
Poached sea trout (p.115)
Potato salad with anchovy
    and lovage (p.152)
Rhubarb, rose and pistachio
    pavlova (p.196)
Cantuccini (p.223)

A SUMMER MENU
Baba ganoush with spiced
    flatbreads (pp.18 & 23)
Green beans, anchovy, quail
    egg and mustard (p.68)
Spiced quail with herby couscous
    and yogurt (p.146)
Middle Eastern(ish) beetroot
    salad (p.163)
Goat's curd cremets (p.198)
Chocolate truffles (p.212)

AN AUTUMN MENU
Scotch quail eggs (p.34)
Warm butternut squash salad with
    labneh and chilli (p.72)
Neck of lamb with roasted garlic
    and flageolet beans (p.130)
Spring greens with garlic, lemon
    and anchovy (p.167)
Honey and rosemary ice cream (p.184)
Brownies (p.216)

A WINTER MENU
Roasted spiced almonds (p.31)
Jerusalem artichoke soup with
    roast onion, mushrooms
    and chives (p.62)
Braised shin of beef with roasted
    bone marrow (p.137)
Glazed turnips (p.164)
Tangerine jelly (p.193)
Date balls (p.223)

A VEGETARIAN MENU
Pea, watercress and mustard
    toasts (p.46)
Burnt chicory, pickled pear,
    Gorgonzola and walnuts (p.66)
Potato rösti with poached duck
    egg and mushrooms (p.101)
Braised radicchio with hazelnuts
    and sherry vinegar (p.177)
Flourless chocolate cake (p.205)
Baklava (p.217)

AN ITALIAN MENU
Ramerino in culo (p.32)
Panzanella (p.71)
Braised pig cheek with polenta
    and gremolata (p.119)
Spring greens with garlic, lemon
    and anchovy (p.167)
Espresso sorbet (p.191)
Florentines (p.214)

A BRITISH MENU
Welsh rabbit (p.42)
Potted pork with pickled rhubarb (p.92)
Poached chicken with peas, onion and bacon (p.142)
Strawberry and elderflower trifle (p.194)
Mini meringues (p.222)

AN AMERICAN MENU
Pork scratchings with guacamole (p.28)
Prawn gumbo (p.51)
Southern-style shoulder of pork (p.124)
Boston baked beans (p.170)
New Orleans bread pudding (p.201)

A SOVIET-ISH MENU
Venison rissoles (p.39)
Soused herring with warm potato and dill vodka (p.84)
Chicken plov (p.138)
Sticky apple cake with drunk currants (p.202)
Salted caramel chocolate (p.221)

A FRENCH MENU
Anchoïade (p.22)
Vichyssoise (p.54)
Pot-au-feu (p.148)
Pear and almond tart (p.208)
Chocolate truffles (p.212)

Index

Page numbers in **bold** denote
an illustration

ACKNOWLEDGEMENTS

I would first of all like to thank my sister Mary for starting the supper club with me and helping to make it so special, and my wife Rosie for, among many, many other things, being team leader in Mary's absence.

All those who have cooked with me at the Secret Larder: Oliver Thring, Alistair Instone, Will Foster, Tom Parker Bowles, Lucas Hollweg, Signe Johansen, Alice Hart, Georgie Fuggle, Shane Osborn, Ravinder Bhogal, Stefan Gates, Danny Kingston, and Pigs in Pinnies Alice Brady and Clara Paul.

Everyone who has helped out for naught but food and grog as payment, in particular my brother Will and his girlfriend Chloe, Tobie Mathew, Lydia Stevens, Ed Hammond, Hero Dalrymple, Meghna Majumdar, Flora Lowther, Sam Gordon, Ed Bacon, Ali Wallace, Dan Evans and Jamie Loyn.

My agents Jennifer Christie and Jane Graham Maw – ever sage, ever lovely.

All the guests at the Secret Larder who have been so wonderful to have for dinner, always friendly, polite, and understanding that, far from being a restaurant, this is someone's home.

Marky Market for delivering the best meat and fish from the markets right to my door, and Andreas Georghiou for his perfect fruit and veg.

Augustin and Hugh at Printers and Stationers for being so instrumental in the reincarnation of the Secret Larder at your beautiful shop.

Edu Hawkins for his Grandpa Elliott on p.140 and for lugging all his extraordinary photographs from Oxford once a year.

The team at Anova Books – in particular Maggie Ramsay who is as sharp and knowledgeable an editor as I could ever imagine; Georgie Hewitt who made this book look so beautiful; and Emily Preece-Morrison who made it happen.

Yuki Sugiura for the stunning photography, Wei Tang for such well-judged prop styling, and Valerie Berry for making the food look so good.